Jamaica
and Me

JAMAICA

AND ME

*The story
of an unusual
friendship*

LINDA ATKINS

RANDOM HOUSE NEW YORK

All rights reserved under International and Pan-American Copyright Conventions. Published in the United States by Random House, Inc., New York, and simultaneously in Canada by Random House of Canada Limited, Toronto.

Grateful acknowledgment is made to Warner Bros. Publications U.S., Inc., for permission to reprint five lines from "Lean on Me," by Bill Withers. Copyright © 1972 by Interior Music (BMI). All rights reserved. Reprinted by permission of Warner Bros. Publications U.S., Inc., Miami, FL 33014.

Library of Congress Cataloging-in-Publication Data
Atkins, Linda.
Jamaica and me : the story of an unusual friendship
p. cm.
ISBN 0-375-50073-1
1. Foster children—United States—Case studies. 2. Homeless children—United States—Case studies. I. Title.
HV881.A88 1998
362.73'3'0973—dc21   97-35113

Random House website address: www.randomhouse.com
Printed in the United States of America on acid-free paper

24689753

First Edition

BOOK DESIGN BY BARBARA M. BACHMAN

Author's Note

Jamaica and Me is the story of my relationship with a young homeless child. In this story I hope to convey the actual life of one child during the nearly two years I knew her. Although it is the story of Jamaica, it is also the untold story of the many other abused and neglected children caught up in a child protection system so overburdened and fragmented that it often fails to protect them.

In recounting this story as I experienced it, I have no wish to expose or point a finger at any person or institution. I have made every effort to conceal and protect the identity and privacy of all people and institutions relevant to the story. All names are pseudonyms. Events that have had to be fictionalized in order to protect the privacy of individuals are nevertheless rendered with the greatest psychological and emotional accuracy possible.

Because my relationship with Jamaica was at all times that of a volunteer to an institutionalized child, I was never privy to conferences about her, nor did I have access to any official records. All information about Jamaica, about her history, and about incidents that took place outside of my presence, was told to me by staff, Miss Pope, and Jamaica herself, and so I cannot vouch for its accuracy. I have related the events that took place in my presence and the information I gathered directly with as much accuracy as the necessity to protect the privacy of others allows.

This book is dedicated to
Jerry Charlos, Samantha, Benjamin,
Evalyn, Pat, and Elly,

My Roots, My Branches, My Loves.

You who have been so vital to me
could not have been kinder
or more generous.
For that, I am eternally grateful.

For several months in 1985, police received reports of what appeared to be a young child, not clearly boy or girl, darting in and out of the subway tunnels underneath the Port Authority Bus Terminal. Such fleeting glimpses were caught of this elusive creature that many thought the obscure form was a wild animal—a stray dog, or perhaps the enlarged shadow of a rat.

This is the story of Jamaica, the child who appeared and disappeared. It is also my story as a participant in her fate and a witness to its cruelty, to her unremitting endurance and bravery, and to the tides of her and our times, which rage with such violence and power that for some it is nearly impossible to keep head above water.

Prologue

Once more my protector arrived. He walked in after the eight-to-four shift smelling of Lucky Strikes and welding fumes. Still in overalls and worn-out work boots, he stood in the doorway for a while, smoking and holding his Irish tweed cap in his hand. I heard his breathing, inhaled his smell, and lay still and mute in his presence and its soft pure comfort, which began to soothe my terrified body.

"Nahni." My father whispered the name that he had given me and that only he was ever allowed to use. "Nahni," he said again, just loud enough for me to be certain it was safe to open my eyes and let hope rise above the slow, steady *whoosh* of the pale green iron-lung tubes that worked on the other side of my ward at Boston Children's Hospital.

I was ten. I was lucky and terrified. Our neighborhood had been flattened by the polio epidemic; some of my friends had died, others were paralyzed, the mother next door now lived in her wheelchair. My fear in the hospital was unbearable. I knew no one; no one knew me. The slow, steady breathing of the iron lungs was my constant and dreaded companion. The watery *whoosh* filled every crack and crevice and could be heard through the hustle and bustle of the day and the quiet of night, and in the deep, dark realm of my dreams. I looked at the heads of the bodies entombed inside those pale green coffins and feared that I was about to be buried alive. At any moment, the aides in their blue sanitary suits, who came around to offer me food with smells so terrifying I could not eat, would take me and slide me into one of those hungry, disease-breathing green monsters. The only part left of me would be my head, sticking out, watching *I Love Lucy* in the mirror above the tube.

During those months I didn't watch *I Love Lucy* or anything else reflected in those many mirrors lined up across the room. I closed my eyes, curled up with my face toward the wall, and waited for my father to arrive, as he did every single day either before or after his shift at the Bethlehem Steel Shipyard, where everyone's father worked, if he was lucky. *We* were lucky; my parents believed we were, and they told me so. My father not only worked but was skilled. Thanks to his Passamaquoddy Indian heritage, he had exceptional balance. He was a rigger who walked the high steel beams. After school I rode my bike to the shipyards near our house, sat on the grass outside the fences that enclosed those huge black steel dry docks, and watched. I knew my father's every move; now, as I lay in bed waiting, I clamped my eyes shut against the deathly sights and sounds and watched him on my closed eyelids, high up like an acrobat, moving swiftly, pounding, drilling, showering the skies with welding sparks, catching girders as they swung toward him from the crane beyond. In my bed, I held my breath while he held his balance.

When my father arrived, I recognized the sound of his walk. He came over to my bed and sat down beside me; once again, I felt my pride and his when I regaled him with tales of the stunning feats he performed, mirrored through eyes fixed on him from my perch below. It was *this* mirror that held me and took me beyond those ghostlike *whoosh*ing sounds, into my father's day and into the certainty that if I lay still and quiet enough no one would notice me and put me into one of those tubes before my father arrived to stop them and to feed me food from home— cornmeal mush cooked by him, the only thing I could or would eat in this horrifying place, where I feared contagion from the hospital, the iron lungs, the people in wheelchairs, everything and everyone who came into my sight.

Whenever she could, my mother came, too. Unlike my father, who stood looking out the window, softly telling me tales of his day, of ships being built, and of the men who held balance against the winds to build them, my mother sat on the edge of my hospital bed, washed my face and hers with a cold cloth, braided my hair, held me close, and cried. It was she who one evening felt me nearly slip away from her. It was she and I to whom this nearly happened, it was she who with uncanny mother instinct pressed her mouth tightly against mine and sucked the choking, strangling fluid from a throat that could no longer move anything along and pumped her own air into lungs trying to shut down and close off against life's breath. She breathed for me slowly, steadily, as though someone had taught her how to breathe for two. She breathed and breathed, holding my tilted-up head tightly against her mouth, until the raspberry sherbet that she and I had hoped I could eat dribbled down our chins and was spat out in purple streaks over the blankets under which I huddled, shivering, in the heat of August.

The police cars called to our house screeched out urgency: sirens roared; lights blazed; we raced to Boston. The spinal tap was conclusive, leaving no room for hope or speculation. I had made medical history: I had two kinds of polio at once, bulbar and paralytic. The daily task my mother had required of me the preceding months, during which she had sought constant proof that her children were still healthy—safe from the death moving in all around us—could no longer be accomplished: I could not touch my chin to my chest.

At the hospital the Sister Kenny method was applied. Huge vats of boiling water were wheeled into my room, and steaming-hot compresses were applied to my arms and legs over rubber and flannel sheets to protect my skin from burning. My muscles did not atrophy; my nerves remained wired.

Whether Sister Kenny was right or not, I still don't know, but by my eleventh birthday I was up and running enough to attempt an escape from the hospital in the Red Acme cowboy boots I'd finally been given after wanting them for a year. I went out the window, down the fire escape, and almost to the street, away from the *whoosh*, free from the TV shows reflected in iron-lung mirrors. I fell down, crawled and limped away, until I was seen by a guard. My boots were sent home. I was afraid that by the time I got out of there they would be too small.

I was one of the lucky few whom the monstrous green tubes did not capture. I did not succumb to the songs of the evil Sirens and go inside. I left the steady, engulfing *whoosh* still breathing on my own. My father threw me over his shoulder and carried me to another wing of the hospital. He warned me not to take up the challenge of spitball fights with the young, quarantined diphtheria patients, who watched and cheered me on from behind an invisible wall in the arch to the ward beyond while I struggled to rebuild weakened, unused muscles. I fought through maze ramps whose railings on each side had been fitted to suit my height and to serve as crutches in my struggle to walk on my own again.

Here I met Nina Nichols. In endless days of physical therapy, her strong hands stretched me, massaged me, prodded me, picked me up, and made me cry. Nina was tall, muscular, with steel-gray hair and a crisp white uniform. She saved the active part of my physical life and secured my future. Nina came twice a day. For months she was the first and the last person I saw. I knew she arranged it that way, so she could cheer me up and get me going in the morning, kiss me and tuck me in at night. Before daylight I nestled into the hands that massaged my limbs while she sang me Irish lullabies. "To put the pain to sleep," she said. I winced and cried with cramps, spasms, and pain so intense

I could not breathe. She never said she was sorry. "Hold on," she'd say in her lilting brogue. "We're coming right along, luv."

After she had worked my arms, my legs, my back, she picked me up, cradled me in her arms, and gently stretched out first one leg, then the other. She slid me down the side of her body until we stood side by side, my arm around her waist, my head resting on her breast. My body wanted to keep on sliding right down into the floor, but her knee held me steady, a little stool on which I leaned until she pushed me along into a tiny step. It was Nina who asked that my red leather cowboy boots be brought back. I needed them, she said—their weight would be useful, a natural asset to physical therapy, a way to build up strength in my leg muscles. Each day after she worked on my legs, she put the boots on my bare feet. I slid down her body and stood beside her in cowboy boots and pajamas.

I was getting stronger. I would now eat food from the hands of two people, Nina and my father. Each morning I lay in bed, awake before daybreak, and waited for Nina to arrive and move aside all the food I would not eat. This food with the scent and touch of strangers, food cooked in huge pots in strange kitchens where odors shot out and strangled you, I knew to be deadly poison. I feared it and never ate it. If I ate it, I would never find my way back, I would never return home.

I watched from my bed for Nina to arrive, unpack the food she had brought for me and move aside all the food I would not eat: the small jars of jam with beautifully painted tops sent to me by the patient down the hall, stacks of cookies and pieces of sheet cake from the kitchen, containers of juice and milk, bowls of fruit cocktail left by staff with the words "You'll be hungry and want something to eat later."

While Nina unpacked, she told me stories of the food I had waited for: thick brown bread spread with butter, cinnamon, and sugar; pancakes and plum jam; crisp bacon and wheat-toast sandwiches.

"I spread this brown bread with as much butter as it would hold without tearing through. We don't want to lose the sugar down the chute. The pancakes are lovely, not too soggy, I waited for them to cool and put the jam on just before I left the house. Your bacon is really crispy today. I turned it over and over until"—Nina unwrapped the sandwich, took out a tiny piece of bacon, and popped it into my mouth—"it was just perfect."

Nina placed my food like a banquet in the place vacated by the poisonous food. While others around me shook their heads and brought me still more poison, I feasted on the cornmeal mush, brown-bread-and-sugar sandwiches, pancakes with jam, and wheat toast and bacon that were my comfort and my life.

"You have my honeydew?" I'd ask to set up our joke.

"If honey do, *then* honeydew," Nina replied, looking over at the food waiting on my bedside table while she pushed me into the seemingly impossible step that would lead to the next and the next. To strengthen and keep my throat muscles moving, I learned to play Mozart on the flute.

Eventually I went home, but my father and I returned twice weekly to the physical therapy clinic. It was then that I met Lina and Anna, sisters whose spines and other parts of their bodies were so deformed by inherited afflictions they were nearly bent in two. Both sisters' skin had formed huge bubbles, which marred their faces and obscured their features so that they looked as though they wore hideous masks. Their eyes were set in tiny cracks magnified many times by the thick glasses both had to wear to give them any sight at all. Anna and Lina were two years apart, but they looked nearly identical, like a pair of grotesque young witches. Their father and mother found them so unbearably ugly that these parents gave them away to the Catholic orphanage at birth.

The sisters were funny and very smart. Books were their friends, so they knew a lot. For weeks that turned into months, then years, we met in the basement physical therapy clinic, where we pulled at weights, walked endless miles, and were stretched, strengthened, and straightened together. They spoke words in real Latin: "Veni, vidi, vici." I answered in Pig Latin: "Enivay, idivay, icivay," until we and our captive helpers gasped with laughter, stopping our breath and making a mockery of the regimes we had to endure. When I turned sixteen, old enough to drive, we had adventures. I was too young to officially take them out of the Catholic orphan school where they had always lived, but when no adults seemed to be looking, we sneaked off the grounds, went to the movies, raced to the Dairy Queen, and, in one particularly daring move, stole off to the Boston Garden, where we roared with the crowd as Bill Haley and the Comets rocked around the clock. I held the stool we had left hidden in the alley so they could sneak back in through their window. If the nuns ever knew of our escapades, they were kind enough to overlook them.

Inside our world of hospitals, physical therapists, nuns, the orphan home, the interior of my old Ford coupé, appearances were stricken from the record, temporarily unimportant. Outside there was no respite, no recovery from the shock and horror that were the mirror held up to Lina and Anna by the world. Intellect and humor could not compete.

We lost touch in the years after high school. I went away to college. The sisters left the convent school and were placed together in an apartment in Boston, where they both attended college. A few years after they graduated, the *Boston Globe* reported their deaths: they had formed a suicide pact.

When I was nineteen, Nina Nichols was murdered. This news filled me with a stark horror I could not shake. That Nina had been murdered was unimaginable—that I would never see her alive again, unthinkable. I could still feel the strength in her arms and hands as she lifted, massaged, and stretched me. I remembered her coming into my room at the beginning and end of each day. She had the will, empathy, and power to keep me laughing and, at my most fragile time, to keep me alive and growing. I wished that the arms and hands that had prevented my muscles from curling into weak oblivion had been powerful enough to fight off Albert DeSalvo, the Boston Strangler, when he entered her apartment, and choked out her life. I mourned her. For many months I dreamt I was walking alone in the dark. I wore a crisp white suit and white shoes. I woke up screaming as I fought and struggled against the arm from behind that encircled my head and held my neck in a vise.

After college I went on to graduate school in New York. My clinical work took me to places I had never been: family court, juvenile detention centers, residential treatment schools, psychiatric clinics. I began to be immersed in the lives of poor, neglected, abused, and mentally ill children. I saw them twisted and buffeted by circumstances that always gave them less than they needed of anything important. I watched them wait for help that would never come, and I saw them try to fashion in their own minds something big enough to hold, soothe, and protect them so they could stay in life a while longer and grow.

I could not speak Spanish well enough to understand many of the people who came for help to the places I worked. So I studied the language on weekends and, after I received my graduate degree, took a job in Honduras to perfect it. I ran a clinic and taught sugarcane workers and their children to read and write. On many days I waited with the children at the slaughter block, where they hoped that someone who could afford to buy meat might slip some meat into their pails, or pour in some blood. And I watched them as a polio epidemic raged out of control and swept through our jungle town, where vaccine was still unknown. In child after child, fever soared, the throat closed up, breathing stopped, muscles disappeared. Here there were no police to summon, no sirens to wail, no painful spinal taps or Sister Kenny treatments or Nina Nichols. The children moved swiftly from life into lines of small white coffins that were carried down dusty streets on the shoulders of men who stared straight ahead. I sobbed with the mourners and stood at the cemetery while children were placed in the dusty earth, and I knew—I had been lucky.

I RETURNED TO New York City. On my first day of work in the psychiatric emergency ward of Bellevue Hospital, I met Jerry Atkins, the admitting psychiatrist. We walked through the steamy halls of the city morgue en route to our first lunch date. We had just interviewed a patient together. At lunch we discussed how to help a disturbed woman who had just tried to poke out her eyes to escape the cruelty of the "Nurse Ratched" on the locked ward for violent patients where she was likely to be sent. Jerry would write a prescription for heavy sedation. I would see her daily. Perhaps she could avoid the horror of being locked in a room with the mattress on the floor, where nurses never came and she would roll around in her own urine and feces. That was the first of the many plans we have made together.

Jerry and I had our own ideas about how things should be done. Both of us had discovered psychoanalysis for ourselves. We were fascinated by its possibilities and eager to begin our own psychoanalytic training. I had applied to the Hampstead Child Therapy Course and Clinic in London, where Anna Freud and her collaborators worked. When I learned that colleagues of Anna Freud ran the Child Development Center of the Jewish Board of Guardians in New York City and that the method and course of study resembled the course in London, I applied to that program and began formal training.

I admired my teachers. German Jewish refugees themselves, they had worked with Anna Freud in London at the time of the Blitz, when children were taken from their parents and moved to the countryside. They had worked to relocate and rebuild the lives of the stranded, shattered children of the Holocaust. They understood how deeply war, loss of family, and social upheaval affect children.

These men and women who had developed the theory and technique of play therapy had the skills, patience, and understanding to unlock the secrets and fears of a child's heart. I watched and listened as voices with heavy German accents brought me knowledge that had been finding its way through the chaos and tragedy of Europe into the English-speaking world. I learned of the powerful communications to be found in the observation of a child at play and that when a therapist understands what is being conveyed, the therapist can engage in play that fosters growth and understanding. I saw how it didn't matter that Spiderman was not a Greek or Roman mythological hero: he might symbolize the magic and strength a young boy feels he has to have to protect himself. I learned that when a therapist knows the symbolism in play, then the parts of Spiderman or Spiderwoman that might be assigned by a child can be successfully and engagingly played by a young woman in her twenties who came from Boston or by a elderly lady with a strong German accent. The knowledge I acquired during the years I worked as a child therapist at the Child Development Center associated with the Jewish Board of Guardians has continued to inform my work.

Later, during the years I worked as a child therapist at the residential treatment school also associated with the Jewish Board of Guardians, I met a mother who looked like Catwoman. She wore very short skirts and high heels, to show her shapely legs. Her platinum hair was cut short and plastered to her head. Her bright red lipstick rose high above her natural lip line. Her eyebrows were thick black arches, painted on. Nothing on her face moved; she did not smile or frown; no facial lines were visible. Her features looked as if they could be lifted off like a mask.

Her voice was pressured, agitated. Why weren't I and the others who worked with her daughter, Lanie, doing more to keep this child away from her? she wanted to know. Lanie was ten then, a skinny, freckle-faced girl who could not sit still. She laughed, tossed her long hair, and looked over her shoulder as she ran away from wherever she didn't want to be, in search of the person she wanted to be with. Often that person was me. I knew she was nearby when I heard intermittent kicks on the wall outside my office where she sat playing alone on the floor. Lanie was waiting for me to walk her back to her classroom, waiting to walk and talk.

Lanie often ran away from the Catholic boarding school where she had lived since she was four. She always ran away to the same place—to her mother, who beat her severely and in fury brought her back to the school. Finally when Lanie was nine the school would keep her no longer. But Lanie's mother wanted neither to give her up for adoption nor to keep her. Instead, she took Lanie to court. The court deemed her a "Child in Need of Supervision," a chronic truant and runaway. She was sent to live at our residential school.

Lanie's mother sat at the side of my desk. She was skinny. "I don't want her near me," she said. "I guess I wasn't cut out for motherhood. It's a good thing I never married or had more kids. Everything she does annoys me—she clings, she whines, she sticks to me. No matter how I hit or punish her, it does no good. She won't shut up. She won't stay at school. She and I are a bad mix. You'd better not let her run away from here anymore," she warned. "If you don't stop her, I'm afraid I might really hurt or kill her."

Catwoman's eyes revealed no expression: no sadness, no remorse.

"We'll do our best to keep her here. Maybe it would help if you could visit some Sundays. We have a van that would bring you up from the city."

"I'll think about it," she said.

She never did visit. I wondered what good could possibly come to Lanie, a child who so longed to love and hold a mother who could not stand to have her around.

I had been just Lanie's age when I learned the details of my own mother's early life. The evening she told me, I moved apart from her—clenching my dish towel, turning my back to the sink where she washed each dish slowly and between words placed it precisely in the drainer. I stood facing out the backyard window, tears streaming down my face, my dish towel too wet to be of use as it tried to stem my tears and hide my embarrassment. I felt hot with fear that my mother would notice. I didn't want her to comfort me and stop her story. I talked to my dog in low tones to muffle and disguise my gasps. I could not bear the knowledge that when my mother was a young girl she had suffered so. I did not want to know that she had been just my age when her mother died. I could not avoid my internal sight of her—small, skinny, a bag of bones—looking, as she said, "just like you do now." My mind took an instant and everlasting photo of her on that train, leaving Indiana to come east to live with her only living relative, her sister, twelve years older. She was all by herself on that train, and so afraid that she curled up behind the drawn curtains of the upper berth and stayed there, hidden, for the two-day journey. She tried to make her box lunch last and she hid her chewing noises behind her hand so those who passed by in the aisle on the way to the dining car would never suspect that she could not afford to eat there too.

As she talked to me I moved down to stretch out next to my dog on the cool red linoleum floor. I hoped my dog's body would hide the shudders my shoulders could not contain. I did not want my mother ever to have felt what she told me about that evening. My mother had felt a childhood of shame—shame at being an orphan—shame that since her father died when she was two, she and her mother had lived in the homes of the people for whom her mother worked until her eyesight and health failed, and my mother had to find a way to do in secret the tasks her mother could no longer accomplish. She felt shame at her well-worn clothing, shame at her skinny body, and shame at the box lunch she carried to sustain her as, alone and invisible, she was hurled east along the tracks in a Pullman car.

Every Mother's Day, when we went to church together and I

held the red rose of the living and she the white rose of the dead, I glanced up at her while we sang. I was hoping not to see the tears that told me what I already knew: I could never give her back what she longed for, what she had lost.

I MARRIED JERRY ATKINS. We moved away to San Antonio, Texas, to treat the casualties of the Vietnam War. Jerry had finished his medical training and, unlike many other conscientious objectors to that war, had chosen to do service as a military doctor. War was all around us. Helicopters landed every few minutes on the pad in front of the hospital. Army ambulances were poised along the pad's edges, engines running; as soon as the dust settled they would roar onto the field, pick up soldiers on the brink of dying, and bring them into the emergency units of the hospital without a moment wasted.

Brooke Army Hospital had the most sophisticated burn treatment center in the country. Daily, young men burned beyond recognition by napalm and other monstrous fires of war arrived from other hospitals, throughout the country, that could not help them. Some soldiers were so fragile they were wrapped in soft white cloth and carried carefully on stretchers along paths that had been constructed for that purpose.

I was pregnant with our first child. My weekly visits to the army obstetrician filled me with dread: I had to pass the burn victims. One day as I walked along the well-manicured grounds, I saw from behind a middle-aged woman walking arm in arm with her young adult son. Arms linked, they were headed along away from me. "I can walk slowly and not have to see this young man," I thought. "I don't have to cut across the lawn, take a detour." Then, suddenly, the couple turned and headed back in my direction. I could not run. The mother was dressed simply, neatly, a cardigan sweater thrown over her shoulders, a skirt, lace-up shoes. The young man in hospital blue had no face. Gold-rimmed glasses gleamed and perched on his stub of a nose. The burning and shriveling had destroyed all his features. I felt the life in my belly move. I fantasized and feared the future. I would not let this happen to the life that moved inside me. I would have to devise a plan.

If war occurred again, I promised myself and my unborn son, I would move with him to the small town in Maine near the Passamaquoddy Indian reservation where my father had grown up. We had spent many summers there. I knew the area. It was remote, quiet, and isolated. I soothed the fear I felt at the sight of the devastated young men all around me. My escape plan would keep my son safe. He would never have his face burned off, he would not have his body blown to the skies. I would buy a gray wig, dark glasses, a wheelchair. I would put a blanket over his knees, a shawl on his back, a tweed cap on his head. I would say he was my ill father. With his blanket over his knees, we would wait out the war together in the backyard of our rented house and read. If anyone came to talk I would say my father had nodded off, was dozing, and I would lure the unwelcome guest into the living room, out of sight of my sleeping father. No one would question me. No one would ask where we got our money, which Jerry would send to us in envelopes bearing no return address.

Our Texan baby was a girl. She went everywhere with us, slept in a car bed under the table while we ate in restaurants, snoozed in a backpack, sat in a bicycle seat, and watched us cross off the days on the "short-timers" calendar as we neared the end of Jerry's tour. We ignored the advice of the army pediatrician who told us to put our hungry baby on a four-hour feeding schedule. We watched and worried as we fed her whenever she was hungry and found for ourselves what was right for our new family. "That guy is putting her on a schedule designed to create a professional military man," Jerry summed up. "I don't think that's what we want her to be."

We returned home to New York City to await the birth of our second child. This time it was Ben, the boy I knew I would hide if I had to.

Years passed; the children grew surrounded by the friends and families of the West Village neighborhood that made New York City feel like a small town. We chose a cooperative nursery school on Horatio Street. To keep costs down, parents volunteered and took turns being the "helpers." The children loved having their parents there, and Jerry and I looked forward to our turns, to second childhoods spent reading the books, playing in the yard, building with blocks, dressing up, cleaning up, and setting up. We sat with the children in the small chairs around the table, to pour milk or juice into our cups, and to eat stacks of graham crackers and pretzels.

This school had a strong interest in child development. Margaret Mahler and her co-workers had done their famous research on separation and individuation with some of the teachers there. I was asked to give seminars for parents and to talk with the principal about four-year-old behavior. As my children grew out of nursery school and began to attend the elementary school nearby, I returned to graduate school at night to study the psychoanalytic treatment of adults. After training, I opened my office, saw patients privately, and taught and supervised candidates beginning their psychoanalytic studies.

One evening I answered a call to my office. A young woman wanted to see me. She had something urgent to tell me. Could I see her right away? Did I remember her?

Lanie rang my bell. The young woman who sat in the chair across from me was nearly twenty-five now. She was obese, bloated, and unkempt. Her hair was cropped short and dyed platinum blond. After leaving the residential school, she got a job as a waitress and moved to an apartment near her mother. Two years ago she'd become pregnant and, although unmarried, decided to keep her baby. She had brought along pictures of a beautiful blond-haired, freckle-faced baby girl. The baby stood in her crib, smiling.

"I could not stop beating her," Lanie told me. "I could not stop myself. Everything she did irritated me. When she grabbed my face or neck, I wanted to choke her, push her off me." Finally Lanie had broken the baby's arm and shaken her so badly the hospital feared brain damage.

The doctors, social workers, and psychologists at the hospital persuaded her to give her daughter up. There was a couple who had wanted her when Lanie hurt her the first time. They would still take her, she said. The day she called me she had signed the papers. This was a chance for her little girl, maybe the last one. She knew she was doing her a favor. It was over now; she would never see her baby again.

Tears streamed down her face. Her body heaved. "You knew me when I was little. You knew, then, all about this. I wanted to tell you what has happened."

We sat together across from one another in big chairs. Her tears flowed. I tried everything in my power to stem my own: I blinked, I nodded, I looked away, I pinched my skin, averted my eyes. My tears would not be stopped. We cried together and I could only whisper, "I'm sorry, I'm very sorry."

I was sorry, sorry for her life, for her daughter, and sorry once again to realize that sometimes it is not what you try to do that holds sway, but what is impossible to undo.

JAMAICA
AND ME

Chapter 1

When I first met Jamaica she was eight years old. She was a skinny, tired, raggedy child with fire-rimmed, pitch-black eyes that glared out from angry slits. Jamaica had been at Mercy Hospital in Brooklyn just short of the thirty days the hospital could legally hold a child without a diagnostic evaluation and a disposition conference to plan for future care. Jamaica had no place to go and no one on record to claim her. She had come to Mercy Hospital for the first time the year before I met her. Picked up living in subway tunnels with homeless crack addicts and alcoholics, Jamaica arrived with no identification, no known relatives, no verifiable history. Once in a while, when off guard, Jamaica spoke of living with her mother in an abandoned apartment near the West Side Highway. Sometimes, she recalled, her mother would wheel her in a grocery cart; at other times she would wheel her mother home in the same cart, dump her out, carry her upstairs, and put her to bed. "I'd sing to her," Jamaica told me, "rock her. She'd always fall asleep then I would curl up in her legs an fall asleep too." If asked directly about her mother, Jamaica flatly refused to speak. "I ain't sayin nuthin, I told those nosy ladies a million times ago."

When I met Jamaica, I also met "Staff." "Staff" was the children's word for the adults who had power over their lives. "Staff" conveyed the interchangeability of these adults, who were not called by name. "Staff toll me this," "Staff say we could," "Staff say we couldn't," "Ax Staff," "Tell Staff," "Where Staff?" Staff ran the ward that was Jamaica's only home and where she was the least favored resident. Staff liked to watch TV. Staff also liked to braid the hair of children while watching TV. Staff did not like to talk to children, or to leave the TV to answer questions.

One fall evening, I walked onto the ward and headed down the hall to the TV room. This was in the mid-1980s, when the devastating whirlwind caused by the arrival of crack cocaine on the streets of New York City was in full force. Crack had become the drug of choice for women. It could be smoked instead of injected, it was cheap, and it made people feel alive and sexy. Daily the newspapers announced and the TV blared out reports of the cruel invasion of crack into the lives of poor children. Children were found alone; they were starved, sadistically beaten, left wet and filthy in their cribs for days. In their rush to get back to the pipe, women abandoned their crack-addicted babies in hospitals. The already overburdened child-protective system was bursting at the seams. There were not enough places to put these children. They were bounced and bumped hither and yon. Overflowing hospitals and child-care centers had to take in more children than they could properly care for; cribs were set up in offices. Images of small lifeless bodies flooded the media; small faces looked up at us from cribs, and there were no hands to lift them out.

This ongoing crisis clashed with my belief in how life should be. These drugs had been dropped like a bomb, creating a war against children. Their childhoods were stolen, their lives ruined. My own two children were nearly grown; one was away in college, the other about to graduate from high school. I missed being with young children, whose particular energy and love affair with the world had always brought me pleasure. I thought my knowledge and skills would be useful to children in this cri-

sis. I decided to enlist, to volunteer, to see if there was anything
I might do.

I contacted Mercy Hospital, where many children were
brought for care. At my volunteer interview, it was decided that
I would work with small groups of girls, children from five to ten.
I would spend two or three hours a week with them—reading,
playing, and talking, or, if the weather was nice, on outings to the
park.

"It will be an exception if you see any one child more than two
or three times," the interviewer told me. "This is a short-term
diagnostic center. The length of stay is not supposed to exceed
ninety days. Only in rare and difficult circumstances, when children have no one to claim them or are so disturbed that it is hard
to find a placement, do we keep them longer."

By early October 1986 I had been coming to Mercy Hospital
for several weeks and had developed a routine. Usually I would
walk down the hall and enter the TV room, where Staff would,
without comment or greeting, tell me who would have the priv-
ilege of going with me for a walk to the park or on a coveted trip
to the candy store. Silently, without looking up from the TV
screen, Staff would point her finger in the direction of whichever
four children she had picked to go. Up to now I'd simply taken
the children Staff pointed at; this evening I had my own ideas.

Several times before, I had noticed a light-skinned tan child,
skinny, with patchy hair in odd-shaped tufts sticking out from
her head. This child lingered on the edge of things. She followed
Staff to the door, followed me down the hall. She walked behind
and to the side, did not talk or seem curious. She watched, apart
from the others, without apparent involvement. She did not join
the scuffle, the tortured pleas of "*I* want to go," "It's not her
turn," "Can I go on Friday?" "You're not fair, you took her twice
already," "Don't pick Charmane, you always pick Charmane," "I
never went, it's my turn." She watched. By now I had noticed
that this child was always there, always by herself. The other
children left the ward for the weekend or ran out to grab my

hand and bring me in to meet visitors, but she was always alone. No one ever came; she never went on a "home visit."

As always, Staff was watching TV. That day, Staff was a large, dark-skinned woman who sat deep into a maroon armchair, her head propped up in back by a bed pillow, a child's turquoise blanket draped around her shoulders. At first I thought she was asleep. She did not look toward the door or acknowledge the raucous banter and bargaining that heralded my arrival. But even though I feared waking a sleeping Staff, I knew I had to speak quickly, before her finger pointed out the chosen children; otherwise, I would have to dispute the choice. That would create havoc among the children as well as increase the animosity of an already unfriendly adult. I stepped into the midst of the escalating fray to rouse Staff and ask to speak with her alone. Slowly and reluctantly, eyes still glued to *Wheel of Fortune*, Staff stepped into the hall.

"I'd like to take the child called Jamaica," I said. "She's never had a turn."

Staff shook her head slowly, silently from side to side. "What do you want her for?" Staff asked. "She's bad, real bad."

"Is there a restriction on her going out?"

"Take her if you want." Staff returned to the ward, settled back into the chair and *Wheel of Fortune*, pointed to Jamaica and three other little girls.

Jamaica raced up the hall. She was practically at the door even before Staff's finger stopped pointing. "It's cold," I told the children. "Go get jackets or a sweatshirt." As the others went to their rooms, Jamaica stood with her hand on the doorknob. "It's not cold, I never be cold."

"Maybe you won't need to wear it," I said. "But I want you to bring a jacket or sweatshirt. It's colder than you think outside." By now the other three were back at the door. "Don't worry," I said to Jamaica, "we'll wait for you." Jamaica ran down the hallway and skidded into her room, her slippery patent-leather shoes like skates on wax. Racing back she fell and began to crawl toward the door, where Staff now waited with a key to let us out.

"I told you she's bad." The words jabbed at our backs while the ward door closed behind us. We walked on newly polished marble floors, past a bronze statue of a mother looking down with love at her infant child, past a temporary exhibit of black-and-white photos of happy children at play, in school, or in the arms of Mercy's beaming, admiring Staff. No sooner had we turned down the avenue en route to Sullivan Square Park than Jamaica broke ranks with our little group and raced into a Korean fruit and vegetable store. I didn't even have time to shout her name before she came running out of the store again and tore off down the avenue, the Korean grocer in swift pursuit. Panic rose as I tried to keep my eye on the direction she was running. Telling the other children to stay in front of the store, I joined the chase, hoping to catch her before she ran wildly into the street and was smashed by a car. When I caught up with the glowering grocer, his strong hand was tightly wrapped around Jamaica's thin arm. Jamaica was clenching something in her fist.

"Give it back to him, Jamaica."

Jamaica laughed and looked the surprised grocer straight in the eye as she carefully placed the stolen goods, the remains of dripping ice cubes, into his outstretched hand.

"Don't come back to my store," the grocer directed me and the girls who had watched from in front of the store.

Jamaica stood with her feet apart, hands on hips. "I no be afraid of nuthin," she hissed at me and at the back of the disappearing grocer. She continued to stare, her head cocked, giving a look of disgust as the girls asked fearfully if we all would have to return now. I replied that we would continue to the park but that Jamaica would have to hold my hand and sit with me on the bench until I was sure she would not run away or rush into a store and take something. "Ice ain't stealin nuthin," she said.

"It is if it's not your ice."

At the park, the three other children raced around, up and down the slide, backward and forward, pushing each other to frightening heights on swings, standing up on the seesaw. Jamaica sat on the bench shivering as it grew colder. She put on her sweatshirt, then mine. I told her I knew one children's story by heart and asked if she would like to hear it. She nodded, folding herself into my side and pulling her hands up into the long arms of my sweatshirt. I recited *Goodnight Moon*.

The cadence of the words spun around us like a silken thread and wove us into a silent soft cocoon. As I said good night over and over to the familiar and friendly characters and objects, Jamaica listened, drooped, then fell sound asleep. The faint whisper of our breathing was the only sound to reveal our presence on the park bench where she cuddled and slept all wrapped up in sweatshirts and a hood, like a sleeping baby in bunting. I held Jamaica and watched the other girls play hide-and-seek among the benches while the sun went down and the park grew black.

We walked back up the avenue through the cold and dark.

"You be gettin you ass in trouble, Jamaica," the others scolded.

Jamaica looked up at me, rolled her eyes in exasperation, and smiled. "You takin me out wit you again or not?"

Chapter 2

Fall folded into winter. Jamaica got more turns to go out with me, because I kept my eye on the rotation. I grew to like her. I admired the way she stood before me and with hand on hip argued and cajoled to get her way. At times her relentless, challenging, confrontational glares made us both laugh. To her delight I nicknamed her Slippery Shoes, because she fell constantly. Unlike most children her age, she hated sneakers; she felt dressed up in the shiny black patent-leather Mary Janes Mercy had provided for church on Sundays. Jamaica wore them every day of the week. Each time she galloped up the tar hills of Sullivan Square Park, she fell all the way down, skinning her elbows, knees, hands. When she fell, Jamaica got up and ran again. She did not cry.

"Slippery Shoes," I said one afternoon while picking her up from a hard, bloody fall, "do you have sneakers?"

Hand on hip, body tilted to the side, she glared at me, a look of pure disdain on her face; she lifted her eyebrows slightly to indicate that this was a question of pure stupidity.

"Well?" I pressed.

She continued her silent glare and sucked her teeth to make

small trilling noises. Her lips curled tightly shut; she clucked with disdain.

I gently pressed a paper napkin to her scabby and bloody knee. I did not want to get into a tug-of-war with her about wearing the sneakers I knew Mercy gave the children. I ignored her ferocious look and announced, "Slippery Shoes, I'm buying you sneakers. You can choose them. I'm not going to let you keep falling down."

Jamaica looked me straight in the eye, then ran off, fell, and cried a little.

When I met Miss Henry, the social worker on Jamaica's ward, she was conducting a meeting with Staff in the lounge. I had been referred to her by the social worker who ran the volunteer program. After about two months, when most of the children I knew went home, to foster homes, or to institutions, Jamaica remained. At her disposition and planning conference it was decided to hold Jamaica at the hospital for the further testing and evaluation needed if the hospital were to find the best placement for her. Jamaica's educational and psychological needs were complex; it was difficult to find a placement that could offer the range and intensity of services she needed.

I decided that I would like to know more about her and if possible become a Big Sister, a volunteer who devoted time to just one child. I had supervised the Big Sister program at the residential treatment center where I worked, so I knew the importance to a child alone in an institution of having one person to count on, one person who'd visit, whom the child could look forward to seeing. Because Jamaica had stayed at Mercy longer than any of the other children I met, I took her out frequently. We were beginning to know each other. I began to dread the times I had to leave her behind to take out new children or children who were at Mercy so briefly they would be gone before I returned again. On days when Staff pointed out other children to go out with me, Jamaica stood apart watching. She did not plead or run up to me. She stood apart and glared. I could not ignore her presence. When I walked down the hall with the others and left Jamaica behind, I felt sick to my stomach, as if I were betraying a friend.

Besides, Jamaica and I had fun. I admired her remarkable ability to make something out of nothing. She insisted we carry lunches in the knapsacks she made for both of us from Mercy's garbage bags, and she waited patiently for me to show up with the food she had asked for, which she inspected item by item before packing it up in the knapsacks and arranging them on our shoulders.

If I became Jamaica's Big Sister, I wouldn't have to disappoint her. There would be no more taking other children out while she watched from the sidelines. The horrible necessity to choose who would go out with me would end. I could take her to do and see some of the things she asked about, things she saw on TV, like the Radio City Music Hall shows or the whale in the New York Aquarium at Coney Island. Each time I left she stood with hand on hip and asked, "You ever be comin back to get me?" I wanted to be able to answer a definite yes.

Miss Henry was a serious-looking middle-aged woman, dressed in crisply tailored suits, who spoke politely and had a no-nonsense approach to her job. When I told her that I would like to change my volunteer job status and become a Big Sister to Jamaica, she listened with interest. I pointed out that Jamaica had remained at Mercy long after all the other children I'd known had left. It was difficult for me to take out new children I didn't know while leaving her behind looking on. When I told Miss Henry how bad I felt at leaving Jamaica behind, she replied, "You're probably more upset about this than Jamaica is. She is a disturbed little girl, calculating and ruthless. She doesn't really get attached to anyone; she only looks for the next hand held out to give her something. But give it a try if you want to. Jamaica is likely to be here for a long time. She is extremely hard to place. We are allowed in exceptional circumstances to keep getting ninety-day extensions of the time a child is permitted to stay here. We are considering sending Jamaica to our group home. It is here in Brooklyn, but there may not be an opening there any-time soon, so she is likely to be here for a few months before something becomes available for her."

"Will I be able to continue to see her once she is moved?"

"Wait and see if you still want to."

This was Jamaica's second stay in Mercy Hospital. The year before, she had been brought into protective custody by the po-lice. She had been panhandling at the Port Authority Bus Ter-minal. She put up a big fight when the police approached her. At first she tried to run away, darting frantically through the crowds of early-morning commuters and down into the tunnels, causing a shutdown of the line. When police closed in from all sides, she was huddled dangerously close to the third rail, crouched down behind a switch box. The cops wore gloves and padded sleeves to protect them: they were afraid she'd bite.

Jamaica was tiny—her estimated age was between six and seven. She had a small face and her scrawny body was covered with bites, scratches, and bruises. Her hair was matted and filled with lice and it smelled of smoke and oil. Her shoes were too big, her clothing too small, her age unknown even to her. Ja-maica knew her name, first and last—Jamaica Thomas. She had a mother, Bunny, who she said was eighteen; they had lived in various places, the most memorable to her being 135th Street, where she said there was a friendly West Indian groceryman who gave her candy and gave her mother cigarettes. Jamaica did not know what happened to 135th Street or where the house was she lived in with her mother by a highway. Jamaica told me that Bunny had lots of boyfriends at this house and that sometimes Jamaica had to undress her, put her to bed, and sing her to sleep. She pretended to read Bunny stories from magazines. "I would read her about places we were goin to live an she would smile an nod an nod an fall asleep. I liked it there, I could do anything I wanted." Jamaica had never been to school.

One day—it was unclear whether this was weeks or months

before Jamaica was found—her mother had what appeared from Jamaica's account to be a seizure. "White toothpaste stuff wuz runnin from her mouth an she fell out on the sidewalk." An ambulance was called, a crowd gathered. Jamaica stood small and silent in the crowded chaos while Bunny was taken away, Jamaica didn't know where. She never saw her mother again.

Inquiries were made of all the Thomas families in the city. None of them were missing any members. There was no one to ask about a friendly West Indian groceryman on 135th Street.

Chapter 3

Jamaica and I had just sat down at a table overlooking the sidewalk in the Bagel Shop at the corner near my home. It was the spring of 1987. In the five months I had known Jamaica we had established a routine for every Tuesday. Mercy held classes for the children placed there; I picked Jamaica up after school. We took the subway from Brooklyn to Fourteenth Street in Manhattan, then walked down Sixth Avenue, stopping for a hot dog at Papaya King or for a bagel at the Bagel Shop. Our walk was always a challenge. Once out of the subway and after we crossed Fourteenth Street, Jamaica left Mercy behind. She began little feints, quick dartings, a short dash toward the grocery store—calculated moves that made me react with alarm and an admonishing "Get back here and hold my hand."

"I'm fast," Jamaica said. "Much faster than you are. You're ol an slow. You could never catch me. My mother wuz fast an young. She could always catch me but you never can."

"You know, Jamaica," I retorted, "you're right. I'm not young and fast like your mother, and probably I couldn't catch you if you wanted to run away, but I can hold on to you real tight, we can go some places together, and"—I made a quick lunge toward her—"I can grab you like this." I picked Jamaica up and swung her around and around. She squealed and stuck out her feet as if she were riding on a flying swing. When I put her down, she smiled, pretended to walk next to me, then made another quick feint. Again I lunged, grabbed her skinny little body, and swung her around. When I put her down she laughed her high-pitched giggle, infectious to the passersby. Then she lay down on the sidewalk and began to roll until I picked her up, threw her over my shoulder, and continued down Sixth Avenue.

No sooner had we sat down on this April day than Jamaica said, "I bet you won't lemme have no coffee."

"You like coffee, Jamaica?"

"I love drinkin coffee," Jamaica replied, going on to tell me how she used to go with Miss Pope and her friends to the doughnut shop and just sit, "talkin, eatin, and drinkin coffee." "I like my coffee with lots of sugar and lots of milk," she said. "Miss Pope drink hers so sweet it be like candy."

"Who's Miss Pope?" I asked.

"Am I gonna have coffee or not?" she replied.

"I don't mind you having coffee. Here, have some of mine, I'll go get a cup and some milk for you."

Jamaica glared. "I wants my own coffee. When I was wit Miss Pope she always say to the doughnut man, 'Two cups of coffee, one for me an one for this little bad girl.' The man gimme coffee in my own cup an I puts in the milk and sugar."

"I'll go get you a cup with a little coffee and you can put in a lot of milk."

"A lot of coffee an jus a little milk is what I have," Jamaica snapped back.

"A little coffee and a lot of milk," I countered as I left the table to ask for a cup of coffee one-third full.

Jamaica peered into the cup, shook her head, clucked under her breath, and began with great solemnity to fill the cup with milk, stirring gingerly after each addition. When the coffee attained just the right color she shouted out "Yes!" and continued her preparations, adding small spoonfuls of sugar carefully stirred and tasted until the brew was satisfactory. Just as she was about to drink, with the rim of the cup touching her lip, Jamaica suddenly stopped, put the cup down, and asked, "Are you gonna tell Staff?"

"I'm not going to tell Staff, and I don't think Staff is going to ask, 'Did Jamaica drink coffee today?' But if Staff does ask if you drank coffee, I will say yes, you did, because you were with me and I gave it to you. I feel the same as Miss Pope—a little coffee won't hurt you. I loved it when I was little. Maybe Miss Pope did, too. It's fun to sit, drink coffee, and talk."

Jamaica stirred her coffee and drank it by spoonfuls. "I like this coffee," she said and, looking around, added, "I like this place. Miss Pope used to make good steak, too—lots of A.1 sauce an lots of onions. We sat together in her big ol chair, ate, an watched TV. I bet you don't make good steak."

"What happened to Miss Pope?"

"We had some trouble, so she sent me here for tests an now I can't go back. She mad at me, real mad—the social worker ax her an she say she never want to see me as long as she live. Thas it."

"Who is Miss Pope?"

"She be my foster mother, I live wit her for a while, she had a little house an I used to sleep in bed wit her when I be scared. But now she mad an say I be really bad an hurt her heart, so I can never see her again. Maybe she be dead or somethin."

Chapter 4

It was May. Jamaica remained at Mercy: another ninety-day extension. I arranged for permission to take her for overnight visits—this despite the warnings of Miss Munroe, a friendly Staff who told me, one evening when I came to pick Jamaica up, more about the circumstances leading to her removal from Miss Pope's home.

After Jamaica had been found at the Port Authority late in 1985, she was sent to Mercy for evaluation and planning. Mercy suggested foster care, and Jamaica went to live with Miss Pope. For the first few months things appeared to go well. Miss Pope was a motherly sixty-year-old woman who had raised two successful children now out on their own. After her husband died, she went back to work, managing a local copy shop. Her daughter and grandchildren lived nearby and visited often. Her son, an accountant, was married, had several children, and also lived near his mother. Miss Pope had a boyfriend, a man also in his sixties.

Miss Munroe's voice was strong, somber. "Don't let her anywhere near men unless you are right there watching. Jamaica is sexually preoccupied far beyond her years; she has been exposed to all kinds of sexual stimulation." According to Miss Munroe,

Jamaica had told one of the doctors of being raped by one of her mother's customers. She had been asleep next to her mother, then awakened to find "a grown man was on top of me, he stuck his big thing in me an it hurt. I was screamin an hollerin for my mother to wake up. She woke up an saw all this blood on me an the man's big thing in me. She started to beat him on his head with this big broomstick. He fell down an my mother kept hittin his head so it wuz all bloody, a mess wit big open spaces. My mother an me rolled the man out the house down the stairs and left him on the street. My mother gave me ice for my booty an lots of white pills that took away the pain. My booty got better but my mother toll me to stay away from the mens that came to fuck. She hid me in a corner in back of some old piles of suitcases, so they wouldn't be tryin to stick they things in me again. I stay real quiet when the mens was there."

Though I wanted to know everything possible about Jamaica's history, I became distracted and began to tune Miss Munroe out. She continued to talk as I recollected an incident that occurred when Jamaica had visited a few weeks before. We had just come in and were preparing to make lunch when loud screams came from the bathroom.

"Help, help!" Jamaica shrieked. "Come on in here an help me, I need you!"

I ran into the bathroom to find her naked from the waist down.

"Look," she said. "Look at my panties." Jamaica was holding her white underpants so that the crotch was draped over the palm of her hand. A bright red smear was centered in the crotch. She raised her hand to within inches from my eyes so that I could get a better view.

I asked if she had fallen, if she had hurt herself in the park and not told me. I looked at this bright red blood smear on the child's cotton panties with fear—what had happened to her?

In her husky voice, speaking to me as though I should have known something so obvious, Jamaica said, "No, nuthin happened. It's the woman's thing, I got the woman's thing, you'll have to give me one of those white sticks to put up my booty."

I glanced around to see the bathroom cabinet doors open, Tampax strewn all over the floor, and the red nail polish brush lying in a pool of pink in the bathtub where Jamaica had tried to wash it off. Borrowing one of Jamaica's favorite expressions, I said, "You're playing with me, you haven't got the woman's thing. It's not time yet, you're far too young."

At first Jamaica protested. She tried to keep up the pretense, telling me she had known kids her age who had the woman's thing and who had babies and always "fucked with mens." But soon she started to laugh and pointed at me and shouted, "Fooled you! Fooled you!" Jamaica *had* fooled me; as we tried (unsuccessfully) to use nail polish remover to take the bright red stain from her underpants, I was unaware of the past and future potential harm that lay buried in her fantasy.

I tuned back in to the conversation with Miss Munroe just in time to hear her say, "Jamaica was brought back to Mercy when she accused Miss Pope's boyfriend of trying to rape her. Jamaica frequently crawled into bed with Miss Pope at night. Miss Pope didn't mind—she understood that a child with Jamaica's history might need extra protection and soothing, and she felt she could comfort Jamaica."

Usually Miss Pope slept alone, but on this night her boyfriend of several years was with her. They were sound asleep when Jamaica arrived and crawled in on his side of the bed. Neither was aware of her presence until Jamaica started to scream, "He's puttin his thing in me! Stop him, Miss Pope, he be puttin that big thing in me."

Miss Pope was terrified. She jumped up and ran over to the other side of the bed and yanked down the covers. Her boyfriend—he fully clothed in pajamas—was waking up, startled, groggy, confused by the commotion. Jamaica was wide awake. Miss Pope asked her what had happened. Jamaica said she'd gotten into bed with them and was looking up at light patterns on the ceiling when she felt something going into her booty. She said she looked down and saw "that thing." Despite Jamaica's pleading to just "forget it," a terrified and horrified Miss Pope brought everyone into the kitchen and demanded that Jamaica tell her and her boyfriend exactly what what she felt he had done to her. Jamaica immediately started to laugh and to say, "I was jus playin, I wondered what you all would do. I was jus thinkin about his thing and I jus said it." When asked about the incident several times over the course of the next few days, Jamaica laughed and repeated that she was "jus playin."

Miss Pope and her boyfriend—he was the father of four daughters and several young grandchildren—worried that something was terribly wrong. And it was dangerous for a child to make this kind of accusation. Miss Pope knew about Jamaica's history of sexual abuse, so she decided to contact the agency in charge of the foster home placement to seek testing and possible psychological treatment for the known and unknown abuses Jamaica had suffered. The phone call Miss Pope made immediately brought the matter to the attention of the Bureau of Child Welfare, whose charge it was to investigate allegations of sexual abuse. Against Miss Pope's wishes, Jamaica was taken away and placed in Mercy Hospital again. As the investigation proceeded, both Miss Pope and her boyfriend had to undergo such grueling and, according to Miss Pope, accusatory and humiliating questioning that they themselves felt battered, victimized, and endangered. By the time the investigation was completed, and the findings substantiated exactly what Miss Pope, her boyfriend, and Jamaica knew to be true, Miss Pope was exhausted, fed up, and traumatized. Jamaica's "jus playin" had cost her a home with a woman who had given her good care, taken her to special remedial classes, drunk coffee with her, and tried to comfort her at night. Miss Pope liked Jamaica. She could see in her an energy and resilience that moved her. She also felt betrayed by Jamaica, threatened by her, and afraid for her family and friends. She said she would never take her back.

Chapter 5

By late May of the summer she was nine, we had received permission for Jamaica to stay overnight with me occasionally on weekends. She looked forward to the visits, so did I. But my friends and family were wary of Jamaica. She was irrational and unpredictable with them. She provoked fear and dislike as she snatched what she wanted when she wanted it, bossed people around, shot angry, insolent glares at those who challenged her or stood in her way. She showed little regard for or interest in anyone around her. Still, the more time I spent alone with her, the more I grew to care about her and to admire her courage. Jamaica looked forward to doing whatever we planned to do. She approached our outings with boundless energy and enthusiasm. She moved me by the intensity with which she appreciated the simple things that generally lay beyond her grasp. The things most children had by right, Jamaica had been treated as though she had no right to have. When given an opportunity, she laid claim to what she longed for. She was urgent in her wish to be clean, to smell good, to have "matching outfits," shiny shoes, her hair braided. At some time in her life she had seen children with housekeys around their necks. She wanted the key to my house—on a silver chain. Jamaica took immense pleasure in knowing she could ask for cereal and there would be milk to pour over it. She looked forward to returning to my house to find all the things she was accumulating there—plastic beads, a rhinestone necklace, a silver half-dollar, colored sneaker strings, tapes of music she especially liked, and the little Nutshell Library books—exactly where she had left them under the lid of the piano bench, which she called "the piano chair." I gave her an allowance to save up for the roller skates she wanted. Each week we put her money into a small basket and added a new note totaling the amount.

Without fail, as we rounded the corner to my block, Jamaica would begin: "Hurry up," she urged, running ahead. "Less go—I gotta see if it's there."

As I unlocked the door, Jamaica would say, "Let me do it, I'm good at doors, I always carry keys for my mother an help unlock the door if she be too sick or high." Once in the door Jamaica dove at the piano bench and opened the lid and spread out all her possessions on the floor. She asked me to help her count her money to make sure the amount equaled what I had written on the little piece of paper. "Nobody be touchin my stuff," she commented as she returned each thing to the bench and closed the lid.

Sometimes when Jamaica and I were alone, she'd play by herself, singing in the tub as she filled it up with soap bubbles, or sitting on the floor trying to put her socks on our big yellow dog, whose tail thumped so vigorously and in such wide sweeps it sometimes knocked her off balance and the two of them rolled in one exuberant boisterous heap around the kitchen. I turned away so that she could not see my tears.

It was Memorial Day, time to open our beach house. I decided to take Jamaica there for a weekend. For almost a month, we planned what we would do. At the top of the list was trying to learn to ride a bicycle. I told Jamaica that she could ride my daughter's bike from when she was Jamaica's age and that we would get special wheels to help her until she got her balance.

"I don't need no special wheels, I can jus ride like this." Jamaica imitated a circus rider pedaling fast, hands held high over the bars. "See, I don't need no baby wheels."

"Maybe not, but just in case I'll get them. I'll also get you a basket so you can ride to the store for me."

The Friday we were to go to the beach I arranged to pick Jamaica up at three. We had talked during the week and I told her to bring her sweatshirt and her jacket and to be sure to bring her sneakers. Friday was beautiful, hot and sunny with a forecast of good weather. I arrived at Mercy just before three, was announced, and went up to the ward. Right away, as Staff opened the door and I walked into the hall, I knew something was wrong. Jamaica and Staff glowered at each other.

"That child is goin nowhere," the angry Staff announced. "Not today and, if I can help it, not any time."

She shot a furious look at Jamaica, who shot it right back.

"Someone like her don't deserve no privileges, she acts like she's so big around here," Staff went on before turning to walk down the hallway.

"What's going on, Jamaica—what happened?"

"I be bad, real bad. I went in my room when you not suppose to an I jump up and down on my bed. You can't do that cause you might kill someone hidin underneath. Staff find me there and say I can't go wit you, that I can't go out this weekend no kinda way."

I told Jamaica to go watch TV and approached the sullen Staff alone. Her story was exactly the same as Jamaica's, with this addition: "You know, we have responsibility for these children— they can't do whatever they want just because they gettin the notion that they special. She talkin about ridin her bike—my kids don't even have no bikes."

I heard the resentment and knew we were in trouble. For months I had avoided responding to—but certainly had noticed—the many glares, the impolite disregard, and the passive-aggressive gestures directed toward me and Jamaica as we went out together. This time I knew I had to do something to address the overt conflict that was threatening to ruin our weekend plans. I was certain it would only inflame matters to argue with this hostile Staff, so I concurred that Staff had a great deal of responsibility and that discipline was important. I added that the plan for this weekend had been made over a month ago and that I hated to see it taken away from Jamaica just like that.

"Next time, maybe she learn." Staff turned her back to me and walked away.

Her rudeness angered me further. I followed Staff into the TV room and asked if there was a supervisor on the ward. She pointed across the hall to an office. The door was closed. I knocked and waited. A tall, attractive woman in an African kente cloth dress and turban opened the door and invited me in. I told her what had happened and said that I wanted to discuss the situation with someone in charge. I reiterated that I understood that discipline was important; I knew very well that Jamaica could be difficult and that punishment was perhaps due. But, I went on, I didn't feel the punishment fit the crime. I told her that I knew Jamaica was counting on this visit, as was I, and that I felt in view of Jamaica's history, taking away something so important to her could prove more harmful than instructive.

The supervisor spoke crisply, directly, with careful pronunciation, her voice without noticeable affect. "That's just it, Miss Atkins—you are the only thing this child cares about, that *is* why we have to take this away. Nothing else will make an impact, because nothing else matters to her." She looked me directly in the eye.

I returned the look and went on. "I don't kid myself—Jamaica doesn't care all that much about me—but if she does care even a little bit, don't you think that's lucky and something to build on, not to destroy? Can't you devise a punishment that will show awareness of the infraction, yet preserve some recognition of Jamaica's need for a relationship? You know I am the only one who has ever visited her—the only one."

"This was too serious; children cannot jump on beds and must not be alone in their rooms. Jamaica knows that. There are too many people involved now to change our minds, Jamaica has to know we mean what we say."

I agreed with her that Jamaica had been wrong. "Can't we all meet to impress on her that everyone is angry, that she has been wrong and that she will be punished for that in some other way? She is just a kid. She is thought to be nine, but no one is even certain of that."

"Nine going on twenty-five," the supervisor said under her breath. "No change is possible."

I glanced at the schoolhouse clock on the wall, thought of Jerry waiting for us downstairs in the car, and realized that we would now be stuck in traffic. I also realized that if I wanted to take this further I had to do so before all the medical staff left for the weekend. I had tried to stay calm and reasonable, but I could feel my anger mounting at the rigid way this was being handled and at all of the staff's gratuitous dismissal of me, of Jamaica, and of any interested consideration of how we might work together to do what was best for her. I knew that depriving Jamaica of this visit would not teach her anything. It would only add to her sense of isolation, injustice, silent rage, and despair.

"I'd like to speak with Dr. Castro. He knows me; we have often worked together. I arranged this trip and promised it to Jamaica. I feel responsible. I don't want to do anything that could hurt her further. Would you please call Dr. Castro?"

The supervisor dialed a number, and after a few seconds said Dr. Castro was not answering. Without comment, she left the room and came back with both Jamaica and the Staff who had met me at the door.

"Sit down, Jamaica," she said. Jamaica looked unusually small in this room of three large women. She did not look at me or the others; her eyes were fixed on the floor.

"Look at me when I am talking to you," the supervisor ordered.

Jamaica looked up; she glanced in the supervisor's direction but kept her eyes averted from direct contact with anyone.

"This lady knows how bad you have been, but she wants to take you anyway. I said you could go this time as long as you say you will never do this again and that you are sorry for the trouble you have brought to us all."

Jamaica sat silently. She rolled her eyes, looked up at the ceiling, and made soft trilling noises.

"Don't suck your teeth in this room," the supervisor said. She glared at me. "See what I mean? This child is not sorry in the least—she doesn't know how to be sorry."

"Jamaica," I said, "do you know it was wrong to go in your room without Staff?"

Jamaica tilted her head a little and nodded a slight, slow, wearily defiant yes.

"Jamaica," I tried again, my voice as firm as I could make it, "remember you told me you should not jump up and down on your bed because if someone was hiding underneath you could hurt them? Are you sorry you did that?"

Again Jamaica nodded an almost indiscernible yes.

To the supervisor I added, "Jamaica and I will discuss this further. I am sure she knows that what she did was wrong, and we'll continue to talk about it. Both Jamaica and I thank you for giving her your permission to go on the weekend."

Fearing that this opportunity could disappear at any moment, I grabbed Jamaica's hand and pulled her up out of her slouch to go. My head was pounding; I felt the fury of my powerlessness in a situation where I was dependent on the goodwill of people who were angry at me and recalcitrant toward me. I thought that perhaps the attention and special treatment I gave Jamaica provoked resentment and jealousy and that Staff wanted my relationship with her to stop, wanted her stripped of special status. Staff treated Jamaica more like a rival than a homeless, disturbed little girl. And I knew that if I said what I was thinking, a meeting might be held in this, Jamaica's only home, I would be adjudged a "problem person," and I might not be able to see her again.

I held Jamaica's hand tightly and jerked her down the hall.

"Less get us out of here," Jamaica whispered.

I stood in silence until Staff arrived with the key to let us out. As we waited together outside the ward, Jamaica pressed the elevator button to take us down. I said, "Slippery Shoes, we're on our way."

"Can I buy a baby bottle to drink in the car?"

We bought a blue baby bottle shaped like a teddy bear and filled it with coffee, milk, and sugar, then joined Jerry in the car. He drove. I closed my eyes and listened to music. Jamaica curled up in the backseat, drinking her bottle, patting the dog. She slept all the way to the ferry.

Chapter 6

On the ferry Jamaica ran wild. She raced up and down the stairwell, slipped out of my grasp, hung over railings until her arms were drenched, stood up on seats to lean out portholes. When a high wave washed over her seat she screeched with delight and then lay close to the railing to catch another. Each time a wave doused some passengers, Jamaica convulsed with laughter, pointed at them as they scurried from the upper deck, and looked around for the next victim. When the brown paper bag containing her belongings shredded in her grasp, she threw the wet clothing into her sweatshirt, rolled it up, and tied it around her waist.

Jamaica loved our little red wagon tied up to the ferry dock. She wanted to ride to the house in it. She rearranged the piled-up bags and suitcases into the shape of a lounge chair and settled on top. "Faster!" she shouted from her perch. "Pull faster—I need to get me a big ol stick."

"Not to hit me, I hope," said Jerry, who was pulling.

"That will get your ass movin," Jamaica chortled. She started to sing the Madonna song "Like a Prayer."

"And yours," the puller replied, to Jamaica's delight.

Jerry's straw hat sat on Jamaica's head. The first time they met, she'd snatched his hat. Jerry always wore a hat; Jamaica always found a way to grab it from his head. Often she bided her time, waiting for the perfect moment. This evening it had come when Jerry leaned over to untie the wagon: Jamaica sneaked up from behind and in one deft movement whisked the hat off his head and flipped it onto her own. Then she strutted off, swinging her hips from side to side. She glanced over her shoulder, waved the hat, and threw him a big smile. Jerry shook his head. Jamaica laughed, pointed at him, and, still holding on to the hat, which I knew Jerry would now let her wear home, she climbed up and settled in.

Jamaica was endlessly flirtatious. Jerry was friendly but wary. In the months I had been taking Jamaica on outings, she had spent afternoons or weekends at our house. She liked to be there—to play, cook, make lunch, listen to her music, play with my children if they were home. She loved to talk to and play with the dog. But on these visits Jerry had observed her in relationship to me and others; he felt pessimistic about her prospects and worried about some of the things she was capable of doing. Stealing was a definite problem—Jamaica stole small and not-so-small things from the house. She admitted to nothing, but I found my daughter Samantha's missing bracelet hidden in her drawer at Mercy one day when we were looking for a clean pair of socks.

Jamaica glared at me when I found the bracelet my daughter had been searching for. "Samantha say I could have it."

"No, Samantha did not say you could have it," I replied. "She has been looking for this bracelet and we are going to give it back to her right now, when we get to the house."

Jamaica was especially happy when Samantha was home from college. They had formed a club, with Samantha's room as the clubhouse. Together they took out all the old dress-up clothes that Samantha had saved—sequined dresses given her by her grandmother, velvet hats and gold lamé shoes, glittery jewelry, gloves up to the elbow. Samantha enjoyed the game, and Jamaica never tired of putting on fashion shows. Together they applied lots of makeup, did each other's hair in outrageous styles, then strutted to music down their makeshift runway into the living room.

But Samantha did not enjoy the fact that no matter how much fun they had together, no matter how often she told Jamaica she could play with the things Samantha had saved from her own childhood, Jamaica would never put back everything she used. Something always disappeared. Even after Samantha and Jamaica carefully replaced all the dress-up clothing and jewelry in the trunk, Jamaica found an opportunity to go back into the room, retrieve what she wanted, and take it. When it became apparent that there might be no end to the stream of things disappearing, both my children requested that locks be put on their doors. It was impossible to tell Jamaica not to go into their rooms—she paid absolutely no attention. When caught stuffing some item or other into her clothing or pockets, she showed no remorse, was angry and defensive, stomped and glared and simply looked for another opportunity to take what she wanted. Eventually we put locks on all the bedroom doors to protect ourselves from her stealing and to try to avoid performing a shakedown every time Jamaica left the house. I had tried to reason with her, pointing out that our kids and their friends were not allowed to help themselves to her things in the piano bench. This fell on deaf ears. Although Jamaica was furiously protective of her own money and jewelry, there was too much around that she wanted; she wasn't able to apply the rules to herself, and, given the chance, she stole.

Despite Jamaica's troublesome behavior, Jerry remained kind and welcoming; the banter he had encouraged between them developed into friendly rituals. And, to preserve the boundaries that guarded against turning fun and comfort into the dangerous sexual stimulation and fantasy that the crisis with Miss Pope exemplified, he avoided all physical contact. We both knew that if we were to take Jamaica home for visits we had to be cautious.

Neither of us wanted to be hauled off for investigation of child abuse. Neither of us wanted to push her away or hurt her feelings, but neither did we want to find Jamaica in bed with us. We could not risk moving over in our bed to welcome a small night visitor in sleepy search of the warm spot where, snuggled in our protective arms, she would be safe from fear and the demons of the dark. This was a kind of solace that Jamaica probably needed but that we dared not try to give her.

I gave Jamaica a little chair in which to watch TV. She could sit on my lap or come to me for a hug, while Jerry had to pat her on the shoulder and tell her he liked to sit by himself. None of this appeared to trouble her. She did not consider subtleties. Once she knew that I was the one to pick her up, hug her, give her what she wanted and needed, she gave Jerry only a cursory greeting, flirted when she could, grabbed his hat, and waved to him in passing. "Jerry always be readin," she observed one day. "He always be sittin alone readin them books—I think he never be havin any fun wit us."

When we finally arrived at the house, Jamaica ran up the ramp to look for the bike. Impatient with my efforts to unlock the shed door, she tried to grab the key. When I opened the door and brought out the bikes, Jamaica put her hand on her hip, tapped her foot, and scowled. She looked first at me, then at the bike, then back at me. She tilted her head back, looked up at the sky, and shook her head from side to side. "I ain't ridin that ol thing." The small blue bike was rusted in spots from the salt air. "I want me a pretty, clean bike—that bike is pathetic." She turned and walked into the house. I continued to take out the bikes and put them in the bike rack outside the back door. Jamaica returned. "Are you goin to get me a new bike or not? I ain't ridin that ugly ol thing."

"It's that or nothing. That's the way bikes get out here, all the bikes are rusted. It happens from the salt air of the ocean. Look at all the bikes—mine, Jerry's, yours, Sam's, Ben's. They're all rusted. None of the bikes are shiny."

Without a word Jamaica took her bike and pushed it down the ramp and onto the sidewalk.

Despite her small size, Jamaica was strong, with long, thin muscles. She could run fast and was agile and coordinated. She was also fearless. Before I could get down the ramp to hold on to the seat, she had seated herself on the bike and was attempting to push off. She immediately fell, skinned her knee, and ended up tangled in the bike with the wheel on top of her. She didn't cry.

"You hold the back," she said. I did, and she pedaled off, weaving from side to side until she steered off the path into the sand and fell forward. "Hold on again." She pedaled forward, lost control, veered off the path, and crashed, collapsing in a heap under the bike.

"You need to practice your steering," I said. "Let's go put the little wheels on so you can ride up and down the sidewalk. That way you'll get the feeling of steering and balance, and then we can try again without the wheels."

Jamaica sat down on the ground beside the bike. She looked up at me, glared, tapped her foot on the ground, didn't say a word. I picked up the bike, picked up Jamaica, and started to wheel the bike home. Jamaica put her head on my arm, whirled around, and before I knew what was happening sank her teeth into my forearm. Hard. I jerked my arm away and grabbed her shoulders and yelled. My arm was bright red, with a circle of white tooth marks. I looked down at it with alarm and dread and was relieved to see that the skin had not been broken.

Most of the time, I was able to keep at bay my fear that Jamaica might be HIV-positive. Although she seemed completely healthy, was lively and energetic, what I had been told was that her history might well have put her in jeopardy; I worried about possible blood exchanges with her drug-using prostitute mother. Or she might have been infected when her mother's customer raped her; she had bled profusely. Even if Mercy knew her HIV status, they could not and would not tell me. After Jamaica took a bloody fall on a picnic one Saturday in Central Park, I'd wiped her knee with my left hand because I had a knife cut on my right. I hoped my fear had been visible to me alone.

Jamaica's bite was painful. I was frightened and furious. The tense discussion at Mercy had left me with a headache. Jamaica was demanding and ungrateful. The bike I had worked on to get in shape was to her eyes rusty and all wrong. Now I had a sharp, sudden fear for my very life. I felt betrayed by her and had to stop myself from hitting her, shaking her, even biting her in return. I threw down the bike, held Jamaica by the shoulders in front of me, shoved my arm in front of her, and kept yelling: "Don't you ever ever bite me! Look what you did! See these marks— you bit me hard and it hurt!" I felt tears of fury and frustration welling up.

Jamaica laughed. She pointed her finger, shook her head, and mocked me. "You mad now, you be real mad."

"You're right, I'm mad, I'm mad at you!" I yelled at her, held on to her shoulder, and stared at her in anger, and in disbelief at the smarting red mark on my forearm.

Jamaica laughed at me again. "You hollerin an yellin like that, but I jus be playin."

"You're not playing. You're not playing with me like that ever, you get it? That's not playing, that's hurting. If that's what you want to do we'll go right home now and sit in the house. I won't play with you if you bite me." Even more furious at her laughter, I shouted louder. *"Do you understand?"*

We stood in silence.

"Jamaica, you better answer me. Do you get what I am saying to you?"

I felt like Staff. I wanted to punish her, get her out of my sight, put her on the next ferry and send her back to Mercy, never see her again.

Jamaica cocked her head, sucked air through her teeth, glared at me, and nodded.

I was in a silent rage as Jamaica and I struggled to put on the training wheels. No words were spoken. She climbed back on the bike, set off, and began to wobble from side to side. She fell off the path once or twice, righted herself, and set off again. For a while, I sat on the fence fuming, and wondering what I was doing here with her. Why did I care about her, I wondered—maybe there was something wrong with me. Jamaica's sudden turning on me had made me feel hopeless and distant from her. Then, after a while, as I watched her bobbing along, talking to herself, veering off the path, falling in the sand, picking herself up, and setting off again, I saw once more her particular fierce determination. This was her opportunity, her first—and, for all she knew, her only—day on a two-wheel bike. Jamaica would do all in her power to learn to ride it. I watched with returning admiration for her spunk. She pedaled past and waved to a deer grazing on the ball field. She fell down again, looked up at me, and waved. My anger softened; I recovered. I waved back and yelled out encouragement. While I watched the rhythm of her effort, back and forth, again and again, I remembered something I'd forgotten: my own thrill when after a whole afternoon of practicing I succeeded in wobbling my way down the sidewalk to surprise my father as he walked up the street toward me. All day I had waited for his return from Sunday duty in the navy reserves, waited and practiced: falling, getting up, starting off one foot on the ground, losing my balance, regaining it, until finally, when I saw him and rode toward him, he stood tall in his navy whites and gave me a full salute.

Soon Jamaica was flying up and down the path from bay to ocean, just barely able to stop when she came to the end. When I told her to slow down at cross paths, ring her bell, and look, she started ringing her bell nonstop at least half a block from every intersection. She learned quickly and yelled for me to look as she flung both hands up over her head. "No handsies," I proclaimed as she rode past.

"No handsies an no footsies neither," she responded, sticking both feet out to the side.

It was early, still light out. I suggested we celebrate bike riding by getting Jerry and riding our bikes to town for ice cream. Jamaica loved the adventure. She ran into the house to get a flashlight and set it in the holder on the handlebars for the trip back. She wanted to lead and positioned herself in front. Just as we were about to set off, the sky over the ocean lit up with forked flashes of heat lightning. Thunderous crashes announced each flare in the night sky. Jamaica's eyes narrowed as she looked up. "Wha's that?"

"That's just heat lightning, it happens in the summer. It doesn't mean it will rain."

"You be sure?" Jamaica wanted to know. "That flashin look real scary to me. Maybe we should be hidin inside."

"It won't hurt us," I said as we set out for town. "It's only heat lightning."

Jamaica didn't want ice cream; she wanted a collection of gelatinous colorful worms, Gummi bears, a pack of candy cigarettes, and a chocolate cigar. "I be havin a baby so I be givin out ceegars," she told me, holding up the shiny gold foil with its purple band.

"How do you know about cigars and babies?" I asked.

"My mother's fren have a baby an he give my mother a ceegar. I have a little puff that make me cough an spit up. My mother laugh an smile at me."

The sky turned dark and ominous. Soon the clouds opened with a burst and began to pour down sheets of rain. We rode along the paths, Jamaica in the middle, between our two bikes and two flashlight beams. It was hard to see, but she rode steadily along in absolute silence and concentration, never veering off the middle of the path into the dark. We arrived home soaked and shivering. I put Jamaica into the steady stream of a hot shower, then wrapped her in warm towels and sweatshirt clothing. She sat in the rocking chair, drinking sweet tea from her bear bottle.

"Can I sleep wit you?" she asked as we headed toward her bedroom.

"No, you can't, but if you get scared you can knock on the wall. I'm right on the other side. I'll hear you and come in." I went into my room; Jamaica remained in hers. We tested it. Jamaica knocked, first hard and then softly. Each time she knocked I acknowledged, "I hear you." She scratched softly, just the tips of her fingers rubbing along the wall.

"I still hear you," I said.

"That be the baby callin you," she replied.

Jamaica wanted to make a cross for the foot of her bed. She took two green-bamboo plant sticks, taped them into a cross, then hung them on the wall. After we said good night and I was closing the door, I heard a husky, admonishing voice call after me.

"And you be sayin it was only heat lightnin."

Chapter 7

At Mercy, Jamaica had initiated a welcoming ritual, a version of peekaboo: When Staff told her I was on my way up, she ran and hid behind the door. I heard the key turn. Staff opened the door. I asked, "Has anyone seen Jamaica?" Most Staff would simply reply no, but occasionally Staff might feel friendly and play along. "I haven't seen that child all day—I can't imagine what she could be up to." I'd moan and groan about how sorry I was that she wasn't there and how much I'd been looking forward to doing whatever we had planned for that day. Then I'd say, sadly, "Now I don't know what I'm going to do. I wanted to go to the movies with Jamaica. Do you have any idea when she'll be back?"

"No idea—I can't imagine where that child is at."

"I guess I'll just have to go. Please tell Jamaica I was here and that I want to see her soon."

All this while, Jamaica would be crawling along the floor to get behind me. Pretending not to notice, I'd begin to walk away. Jamaica's arms would encircle my ankles; I'd shuffle along, pulling her weight.

"What is wrong with me? I can't seem to walk straight today."

"Got ya, got ya!" Jamaica would shout. "I know you glad I'm here. You don't have to be goin home by you own self."

"I *am* glad you're here, Jamaica—you had me scared."

But the next time I went to pick up Jamaica after the weekend at the beach, there was no game. Jamaica was really gone.

When Staff told me that Jamaica no longer lived at Mercy, I looked around the hallway and knew it was true. No skinny little girl was crawling along the floor to pounce on me or grab my ankles. Jamaica had been sent to the group home, I was then told. I had talked with her the night before she left, and she had had no idea of what was about to happen.

I stood there furious. Afraid of just such a sudden disappearance, which would make me another person who simply vanished from Jamaica's life, I had asked Miss Henry to keep me informed of any decision about her. She'd assured me she would, and I had given her all my phone numbers. But no one had called.

I waited silently in the hallway outside Miss Henry's door. I felt my temper rising, but I knew it would be both unwise and futile to blow up as I was tempted to do. I needed to find Jamaica.

"We had an opening in our group home," Miss Henry said when I sat down in her office. "Jamaica was sent there three days ago." She said this matter-of-factly, as though we had never spoken.

"How come you didn't tell me? I would have tried to go there with her, or at least I would have told her that I knew where she was going and I'd be coming to see her as soon as I could. Did you think I would just vanish with her?"

"You're neither her guardian nor her relative, Miss Atkins— that is who we inform. You're a volunteer. Do you think this really matters to Jamaica? I don't think so—I don't think anyone really matters to that child."

"Miss Henry, you said you'd inform me before Jamaica was sent anywhere. Whether or not it matters to Jamaica I can't say, but it does matter to me. I told you so. I thought you agreed that this was important. Is your point that because I am a volunteer I have no importance in Jamaica's life? There is no one *but* me to inform about Jamaica, no guardian, no relative. If your point is what I'm called, that is not in the spirit of what we agreed upon."

I was growing angrier and more confused at the same time. I saw clearly that my efforts were being undermined—that neither the professional staff nor the child-care staff had been willing to try to help me maintain and nurture the connection I was trying to forge with Jamaica. The more time I spent with Jamaica, the more resolute I had become in what I felt was a simple and straightforward plan, a plan with which I felt no human being, let alone a professionally trained child-care worker, could possibly disagree. I wanted Jamaica to know that she was no longer alone in the world—that someone knew her, liked her, and would stand by her. I intended to be that person until she was settled into a decent, permanent place and had something and someone she could call her own. Now I was tempted to ask Miss Henry whether she had ever studied child development and why she wanted to do this work, but that would be trouble and would do nothing to change the fact that Jamaica had been sent away three days ago and no one had let me know.

The longer I was involved with Jamaica, the more I began to feel that the dislike and callousness I had seen directed toward her were now being directed toward me, too. Staff's indifference was not benign but hostile. I wondered if being low person in the pecking order was contagious. If I had done something to offend Staff, it was not obvious, nor was it pointed out to me. I'd seen Jamaica be nasty to Staff in my presence; perhaps that contributed to the resentment. I also knew that I might appear to Staff as though I were a "lady of leisure"—someone who did not have to work, someone who never had hard times. Every time I came to pick up Jamaica, we were off on an outing, off to do something fun, while Staff had to remain at work. Once, when I was leaving to go on a trip, I asked Jamaica what she would like me to bring back for her. Staff, who was sitting nearby, injected herself into the conversation: "I'm the one you should be bringing something back for. I have to put up with her."

"Yeah," Jamaica was quick to respond, "but you not be the one she like."

I could not discount the possibility that Staff's hostility and passive-aggression had racial undertones. All of the Staff and child-care workers on Jamaica's ward were black, and I am white. Staff often seemed much more determined to convey their hostility to me than to offer any real help to Jamaica. Whatever the reason for this unpleasantness and sabotage, I was not used to being treated so badly. It tapped into what my mother called "your nature." It got my Irish up.

"Is there a social worker at the group home, Miss Henry? I want to speak to Jamaica."

Miss Henry wrote a name and phone number on a piece of paper. Once again I walked down the long hallway behind the Staff who had the keys to let me out. I would have loved to race off into the rooms, jump up and down on the beds, and hurt whoever was hiding from me underneath.

This time I crossed the street and went down into the subway alone.

I CALLED AS soon as I got home. Loud music filled the air on the other end of the receiver.

"May I speak to Jamaica Thomas?" I asked.

"Jamaica who?" a heavily West Indian–accented voice inquired.

"The new child, been there about three days." I hoped this really was the group home in Brooklyn—that Miss Henry had given me the correct number. "I'm a friend of hers, her volunteer from Mercy. I want to tell her that I know where she is and I am beginning to make arrangements to see her. Are you Staff?"

"Yes, I am. I'm Ozzie, night Staff. Let me get the child."

The voice was pleasant, comfortable, and accommodating. The music was lowered as she called out, "Jamaica, telephone. Come right here, child."

"Hello."

"Jamaica, this is Linda—is this you?"

"Uh-huh."

"When I went to Mercy to get you today I found out you had gone. At first when I didn't see you, I thought that you were hiding on me again, but when I went to walk away and there was no one tugging at my feet, I knew you were really not there. Staff told me you had gone to the group home in Brooklyn."

"Uh-huh."

"I want to talk to your social worker there so I can visit you. I'll call her tomorrow when she will be in her office."

"Okay. Bye."

"Jamaica, don't say good-bye yet. What are you doing?"

"Watchin TV."

"Are there other children there?"

"Uh-huh."

"How many? What is it like there?"

"It's okay. Miss Ozzie say I have to go. Bye."

"Don't hang up. Let me speak to Miss Ozzie."

"Hello, this is Ozzie speaking."

"How is Jamaica doing?"

"I just come on at night—I haven't seen her much. I did get a report to watch out for her, because she has been fighting with the other children. She bit one of the girls. Best you talk to the social worker or day Staff—they can tell you more. When I'm here they are mostly asleep."

I hung up. Another labyrinth to negotiate, just when we had begun to know the dead ends, the right and wrong turns of the one we were in. I could not imagine what Jamaica was feeling, and I knew she neither could nor would ever say. I could only try to fathom what it was like for her, at nine years old, once again to find herself with strangers, once again to sleep in a strange bed without any idea of a person or place she could even dream belonged to her.

I had seen Jamaica turn to stone before. Her "uh-huh" was a dead sound, the only life left in a blank face with emotionless eyes that stared off to the side. Nothing else would come from her at those moments. "Uh-huh" was the last flicker of connection as she slid into withdrawal. It was an unmistakably off-putting signal, a clear statement that Jamaica had no interest in pursuing the conversation further, had no energy for it. "Uh-huh" was a stop sign.

I first experienced "uh-huh" when I tried to talk to Jamaica about Reggie. One day shortly after I'd begun to take her out alone, I came to pick her up and found she wouldn't talk to me. My greeting, my questions—everything—met complete silence. Jamaica neither looked up at me from the TV nor responded to any conversation. The only sound she uttered was a rote "uh-huh" when I asked if she wanted to go outside. She didn't move, look up, or respond at all except to make this disembodied sound. Though I might have read anger into her impassive look and body language, I felt no strong emotion emanating from her, no explosive, churning rage that showed she was embroiled in battle. That, I had seen before. This was different; this behavior seemed more deadening, more likely to lull to sleep than to provoke attack.

Staff told me that Jamaica was just pouting, that she had refused to talk for two days because she hadn't gotten her way. Staff described an incident that had occurred two days earlier: A "crazy man" had come to visit Jamaica. According to Staff, this man stood on his head in the visitors' lounge and was trying to teach Jamaica to stand on her head, too, when security guards intervened and asked him to leave. The man refused, made a fuss, and had to be forcibly removed. Jamaica also made a fuss—she kicked and screamed and had to be forcibly brought back upstairs.

"Who was this man?" I asked. "Where did he come from?"
Staff shrugged; she had no idea.

I was surprised to hear about this incident and I wanted to
know more. Jamaica had not mentioned any other visitor to me.
I wondered if someone had come looking for her—perhaps her
father, or another relative, or someone else who might want to
see her or might have some information about her past.

"Did anyone talk to him?" I asked. "Did anyone get his name,
find out his connection to her?"

Again Staff shrugged. "Ask Jamaica—maybe she'll tell you
something. I think all the commotion happened before anyone
got a chance to talk to him. He just left."

I looked down at Jamaica, who sat glowering, her face stony.
"Come on, Jamaica," I said, "let's go out for a little walk."

Jamaica didn't budge. I walked closer and whispered, "How
about a cup of coffee?"

Not a flicker.

I took Jamaica's hand in mine and pulled her up from the chair.
She offered no resistance. We walked in silence down the hall.
The sound of the key in the lock signaled our leaving as Staff
opened the door. We went downstairs and out into the late-
afternoon sun. When we got out of the subway, we held hands
again but did not speak all the way to the Bagel Shop. After we
were seated and Jamaica had finished preparing her cup of coffee, she announced, "I be knowing that man Staff say is crazy.
Thas Reggie, my mother's fren. He live with us on a Hundred
and Thirty-fifth Street and he know how to stand on his head,
on his hands too. He teached me that an how to skate. He be real
nice, he ain't crazy."

Jamaica sat looking down into her coffee. She stirred it slowly,
watching it move around and around. She stopped stirring,
looked up at me, and announced, "Thas it, I ain't talkin about
this no more."

When we returned to Mercy that day, I sent Jamaica to go
watch TV; then I walked down the hall and knocked on the door

of the Staff office. I wanted to know what had happened, and I felt hopeful—maybe this visit had provided a lead and we might trace this man to see if he knew anything about Bunny or where other relatives of Jamaica might be found. The Staff in charge described the incident. She had been the chaperone the day Reggie visited and had seen the entire thing happen.

This had all begun, she told me, a little over a week ago, when Jamaica went on a group outing to the park. She looked up from playing and spotted this man, Reggie, in the distance. Happy to see a familiar face and eager for information about her mother, Jamaica left the group and raced over to him. She screamed and yelled with glee as he picked her up, hugged her, and tossed her into the air. Then a panicked Staff ran up to them and pried the unwilling Jamaica from his grasp. Homeless himself, Reggie knew nothing about Jamaica's mother. He told Staff in the park that he was a cousin who had lived with Jamaica and Bunny on 135th Street, just as Jamaica later told me. He asked when and where he could visit Jamaica, and when she left with the other children he told her he would come to Mercy to see her. No one believed this would happen, but as it was apparent that he knew Jamaica and that he might hold some clue to her background, it was agreed that should he come, he would be allowed a chaperoned visit.

A week later, Reggie did show up. Dressed in dirty clothing and carrying a shopping bag that served as his suitcase, he introduced himself as Jamaica's cousin and waited in the visitors' lounge for Staff to bring her downstairs. When Jamaica and her Staff chaperone arrived, Reggie was standing on his head, the contents of his upside-down pockets strewn all over the floor. Jamaica, delighted to see him, quickly joined him in this position.

Then, Staff reported, Reggie began to "show off."

"You be remembering what I teached you, child!" Reggie exclaimed as he and Jamaica stood upside down, eye to eye.

"I can still do them splittos, too," Jamaica replied. She scissored first her right and then her left foot forward, her lithe body in perfect balance. "Show me you splittos, Reggie—show me you one-hand splittos."

Staff called for Security reinforcements as Reggie proceeded to hold one arm out in front of his body and scissor his long legs back and forth in the air.

"Stop!" Staff ordered. "You're going to fall and crush her."

Both Reggie and Jamaica ignored Staff, preferring to go on with these and other exploratory gymnastics. Finally, after several requests and a lot of yelling, which escalated to curses and threats on Reggie's part, he was told he had to sit down at the table or leave. Instead, he sat on the floor in a yoga position. Jamaica sat beside him. Staff would not permit this. When she tried to make Jamaica get up off the floor and sit on a chair, Jamaica bit her hand. Reggie laughed and encouraged Jamaica in her battle. Security at last arrived, and the visit was abruptly terminated.

After Staff finished telling me all this, I left her office and walked back down the hallway and into the TV room to say good-bye to Jamaica. She was curled up on the floor, withdrawn and nearly asleep. I tapped her on her shoulder and said, "Walk me to the elevator, I want to tell you something."

Slowly and reluctantly, Jamaica stood up and began to walk with me. "Staff told me all about what happened with you and your friend Reggie when he came to visit you. I'm sorry that happened."

Jamaica stopped abruptly and looked up at me. "I never had no chance to say good-bye to Reggie, to see what he brought me or nuthin else. You think he be comin back to see me?"

Reggie was never seen again.

I wished there had been a way, perhaps in some other place, for Jamaica and Reggie to sit together in yoga positions on the floor, stand on their heads in perfect balance, do splittos, and chat about old times.

Chapter 8

Three weeks and a few more phone calls after I learned Jamaica had been sent to the group home, the social worker said I could come visit. It was a hot, humid summer day when I arrived in Brooklyn. Fire hydrants were open; children darted to and fro across the street, dangerously close to the passing cars, which drove down the block at a snail's pace. Women—mothers, aunts, grandmothers—watched the children and shouted out curses and commands. Number 153 was one of a block-long line of two-story brick row houses, all with decorative stoops, where it seemed the entire neighborhood sat. I was the only non-Hispanic white person in sight. Most of the residents were black, but I saw a few Hispanic people, and occasionally Spanish conversation drifted through the air. In front of 153 a line of little girls about ten years old practiced an elaborately choreographed dance to a Donna Summer song. They moved forward and backward, spun and turned in unison, paying dead-serious attention to the calls of their twelve-year-old leader, who stood in front demonstrating and correcting anyone who faltered or moved in the wrong direction. They were fun to watch and seemed nearly ready to perform somewhere. These girls, the group home's downstairs neighbors, were the children of an extended family whose door you passed on the way to the stairs. They never played or danced with the children upstairs, I learned later.

I had obtained permission for a "limited visit." I could take Jamaica for a walk in the neighborhood but could not stay for more than two hours. She would not be allowed to go out with me for the day or to visit me overnight until she earned these privileges. I'd been told Jamaica was "not making a satisfactory adjustment." She did not cooperate with night or day Staff, she threw her belongings all over her room, she did not listen to instructions, Staff said she pretended to be deaf when spoken to. Staff did not like Jamaica—they found her difficult and shrewd, always plotting and untrustworthy. Other children's belongings were missing, and Jamaica was the suspect. Jamaica complained when asked to do required chores, such as setting the table. Most often she would abandon the task and wander off to do something else.

I picked my way through the group of women sitting and drinking sodas on the hot, sunny stoop and rang the top buzzer. The noise of the early-afternoon soap operas drifted down the long narrow staircase I could see through the small framed glass triangle cut in the solid wooden door. I rang again and, when there was no response, rang a third time and listened to see if I could tell whether the bell was sounding. When I held the buzzer down and heard nothing, I decided to shout up through the open window, where plaid curtains hung out catching the occasional puff of breeze.

"They're up there," one of the women said in a desultory way. "Haven't gone out all day."

"Jamaica!" I yelled up. "Jamaica, it's Linda—are you there?"

Three girls looked out the window. They saw me, waved what I thought was acknowledgment, and disappeared. I waited outside the front door, thinking that Staff was on the way down to let me in. When no one had appeared after about ten minutes, I decided to try again.

"Hello—anybody upstairs?" I yelled, knowing that everyone had gone back to the TV I could hear playing loudly through the window. "Jamaica, come to the window—are you there?"

This time Jamaica appeared. She looked down through the safety bars of the window and, with a puzzled scowl, asked, "What you doin here?"

"I've come to visit you—go get Staff to let me in."

In a few minutes I heard footsteps coming down the stairs. A very obese black woman dressed in a T-shirt and slacks appeared at the door. I introduced myself and told her I had permission from Miss Clark, the group home's social worker, to visit Jamaica. She invited me in, looked through her desk, and told me she had no note or other information about my visit. Because it was Friday, she said, there was no possibility of contacting Miss Clark. She suggested that I visit with Jamaica at the home, then contact Miss Clark on Tuesday, when she actually spent the day there. She was pleasant, and since this seemed to be the only option, I took it.

In the living room, all the girls were sitting around the TV watching *General Hospital* and coloring. The woman who had let me in introduced herself as Betty, sat back down in her chair, and returned to the program. It was obvious that I had intruded on the afternoon soap-watching activity, so I sat down on the couch and watched, too. Occasionally one girl would ask another for a certain crayon or hold up the Barbie picture she was coloring for the others to comment on. There was the scratching of crayons, the drone of *General Hospital*, and the sound of Donna Summer singing as the little dancers on the sidewalk below squealed and clapped in unison.

Jamaica did not acknowledge my presence. She lay on her stomach, eyes glued to *General Hospital*. In silence everyone watched what appeared to be—to judge by the attention directed toward it—the most fascinating program in the world.

I had anticipated that in a group home there would be "parents" who lived with the girls and ran the home. This was not the case. The group home was run by Staff, who rotated on eight-hour shifts: eight A.M. to four P.M., four P.M. to midnight, and midnight to eight A.M. The Staff who put a child to bed would be leaving about the time she got up for breakfast. The Staff who saw a child off to school would more than likely not be there to greet her when she came home.

At the time of Jamaica's stay in the group home, there were five other girls between the ages of eight and fourteen. When I began to know them a bit, I learned that most of them had been in several foster care placements which for varying reasons had not worked out. Most of them attended special education classes at a neighborhood school. All had spent more time in school than Jamaica, whose only experience with education had come during her brief stay with Miss Pope and in the special classes held for children in custody at Mercy.

The group home's Staff had their favorites among the children. Everyone's favorites were two Hispanic sisters, aged fourteen and eight. They were beautiful girls, tall and lean, with light tan skin and long black curly hair. They dressed attractively, sometimes identically, in pretty cotton dresses and matching shorts-and-halter outfits that they had brought with them. The older girl, Luz, never let the younger one out of her sight and would take on any and every threat. No one was allowed to take her possessions or to pick a fight with her. Sitting on the floor, the sisters would color the same picture, talking softly to each other in Spanish and deciding together what colors they wanted to use. With pride, Staff showed me the room they shared and kept impeccably neat and organized, with their dolls of starched lace sitting prettily on their carefully made beds. The consensus was that they did not belong there. Staff worried about the corrupting influence other girls, such as Jamaica, might have on them, so they were allowed and even encouraged to keep to themselves and to keep apart.

Ozzie McDaniel told me that these girls had had bad luck. Before that they had had what none of the other girls in the group home had: a mother who loved them. The bad luck occurred when a vindictive or jealous neighbor called Child Protection to report that Mrs. Hernandez was a heroin addict incapable of caring for her two daughters. The investigation that followed determined that indeed the mother *was* a heroin addict, but she was anything but incapable of caring for her daughters. The girls were well dressed and well fed; the house was neat and attractive; and both girls not only went to school regularly but were in gifted programs. For many years Luz had had an arrangement with her mother to take a certain portion of the welfare check and manage its spending so that groceries were bought and bills paid. This system had worked for the family and had now been brought into the group home, where Luz managed life's details and problems for her younger sister. Though they weren't abused or neglected, the children could not be left in the care of a known heroin addict, so they were living in the group home until their mother completed a detoxification program. After that they would be returned to her.

Mrs. Hernandez visited every day. Sitting in the bedroom, she and her daughters talked over the best way to get through this time apart. Staff was sympathetic; they liked this lively, attractive young woman, who loved her girls and showed up daily to look after them. They could put themselves in her shoes. They resented the interference that had caused this family to be split apart. They granted the girls little extras—letting them call their mother before going to bed, warming up the special food their mother cooked for them, and letting them eat apart from the others. The sisters took no special advantage of this favored status. They kept to themselves, listened to their mother, and waited to go home.

"WHA'D YA BRING me?" Jamaica asked when the soap was over and she looked up from the TV to acknowledge my presence.

Betty looked at her with disapproval and shook her head. "With that attitude, if I were her, I'd bring you nothing."

Jamaica tilted her head to one side, looked Staff in the eye, and glared.

I asked Jamaica to show me her room. She led me to the back of the house, to a nice-sized room with new blond furniture, matching twin beds, a dresser set, and a child-sized desk and lamp, where both girls were supposed to do their homework.

"Well, did you bring me somethin like candy or food?" Jamaica asked.

I told Jamaica that I had not, that I had planned for us to go for a walk in the neighborhood to get an ice or some candy, but that the social worker had not passed on this plan to Staff, so we couldn't go out until next time. Jamaica stood with her hand on her hip, glaring, with narrowed, disapproving eyes. Then she showed me the shredded remains of a Peter Rabbit book we had bought together when she was at Mercy. "Ripped up in a fight," she explained. Another child had been reading it and wouldn't give it back when Jamaica asked. I looked at the few remaining unripped pages. When I offered to read the book, telling her we could put in the missing parts, she said she wanted to watch TV and left the room. I joined her in front of the TV, where Staff and all of Jamaica's housemates were still sitting.

Oprah produced considerably more animation and engagement than *General Hospital* had. I sat through a few comments on the guests, all of whom had married someone at least thirty years younger, then said good-bye to Jamaica and told her I would speak to the social worker so that we could go out for a walk. I asked her to stand at the window to wave good-bye.

"Do I have to?" Jamaica wanted to know.

"You have to," I told her. "When a friend comes to visit you, you should always say good-bye and, if you can, wave to them. I'll wave to you, too."

I left everyone watching *Oprah*, went down the dark, creaky stairs, and let myself out the door. The stoop and sidewalk were empty; the dancing children were gone and few people were sitting outside. The sun was low in the sky, giving the street a soft, calm hue. When I looked up to the window, I saw a small skinny silhouette hiding behind the blowsy curtain.

I waved up at the window. "Bye, Jamaica."

The form did not move. I waved and tried again. "Bye, Jamaica!" I yelled up to the window.

Again no response. This time I remembered our game. "I wish Jamaica was there to wave good-bye to me, but I guess she's not here today."

I saw the curtain rustle slightly and then, with a jerk, Jamaica pulled it back to reveal herself and to say, "I'll be seein ya—call me up this week an bring me candy, don't forget."

When I got into my car I looked up. Jamaica was standing wrapped up in the plaid curtain. She was completely invisible except for one small hand sticking out through a tiny hole and continuing to wave good-bye.

Chapter 9

After a while Jamaica was permitted to leave the group home for a walk or an afternoon movie, not so much because her behavior had improved as because Staff was glad to be rid of her. She continued to cause trouble with her fighting. Her reckless abandon while running or climbing had led to a bad fall and a trip to the emergency room for stitches. Also, she had developed the habit of standing in front of the TV and refusing to move when other children were trying to watch. When they protested, she would laugh, dance around, and sing into an imaginary microphone. This behavior constantly disrupted the otherwise peaceful TV viewing. Staff would remove her to her room, but she refused to stay there.

One afternoon, Miss Ozzie told me that Jamaica's status in the group home was beginning to look precarious. She said that all the children—except Jamaica—attended a morning recreation program. Jamaica had been expelled for fighting and biting a child so hard on the arm that blood was drawn, requiring a tetanus shot.

Jamaica's fighting seemed to flare up randomly. I thought it had more to do with Jamaica's limited ability to tolerate any kind of frustration than with aggression directed toward others with whom she was having conflict. Jamaica was taken back to Mercy for a day of psychological testing. Brain damage was suspected; did Jamaica have some of the emotional and intellectual deficits often specific to babies born addicted to crack? Because so little was known of her background, however, it was difficult to judge from the results of testing which of her troubles were physiological and which psychological. As far as the group home was concerned, Jamaica was a thorn in everyone's side. She was always disrupting an already difficult environment, and there was a movement afoot to find another placement for her.

One day Jamaica asked what I was going to get her for her birthday.

"When is your birthday?"

"Nest week," Jamaica replied.

"What's the date?" I asked.

"On Tuesday when you visit. I want to have me a party with food and a cake."

Jamaica went on to tell me that Nida, the younger of the Hispanic sisters, had celebrated her birthday at the home. Her mother made fried chicken with rice and had a big cake with creamy white frosting and red roses that you could eat. All the girls and Staff went to the park with Nida, her sister, and her mother. They had a picnic, and then Mrs. Hernandez gave all the girls nail polish and lipstick and helped them put it on. It was like a beauty parlor. They sang "Happy Birthday" to Nida, and she opened lots of presents.

"What I want is what she got," Jamaica said directly. "White skates with pink wheels."

Jamaica didn't really know the date of her birthday, of course—neither the month nor the day of the month. No one knew. I wondered what was usually done about a child's birthday when her birthdate was unknown. Birthdays are not something that should be celebrated on a whim. Usually children look forward to their birthday, plan their party, and make lists of what they want. It was obvious that Jamaica was asking for a party because another child had had one. It was also true that she could not plan for or look forward to the time of her own party. No one could tell her when it should be.

I told Jamaica I agreed that she should have a birthday party, and I said I would talk with Miss Clark so we could decide on a day. We could plan the party together, choose food and a cake, and decide where it would be.

"I want to go skatin on my new skates," Jamaica replied. "An have strawberry shortcakes."

"What skates, Jamaica?"

"The ones with pink wheels that I am goin to get from—" She straightened her arm and pointed her finger three times in my direction.

Miss Clark agreed that Jamaica should have a birthday party, so I immediately invited her. Further investigation by the Bureau of Child Welfare had not turned up any new leads. Jamaica's origin remained completely unknown, her birthdate a mystery. I had never imagined I would have to pick a date that would become someone's birthday. In my family birthdays were almost sacred; they were packed with ritual. The day would begin with one minor present left by the birthday person's bed, to be opened upon waking. Other presents would be opened at dinner, for which the celebrant was allowed to choose the menu and request a favorite dessert. The number of candles had to be exactly correct, whether for a child or a grandparent of one hundred. Birthdays should be with you for always, and to make up a birthday seemed dishonest.

I suggested we tell Jamaica that we would celebrate her birthday on August 28, two weeks from the Saturday of the present visit. I chose August 28 for no other reason than that it was the first day I would be free to give the party. Miss Clark had some feeling for Jamaica—she admired her singing voice and had begun to teach her the songs she sang in her own church choir—and she and I agreed that this date should and would be noted in Jamaica's chart. Unless something was learned to contradict it,

August 28 would become Jamaica's birthday, a day she could celebrate and call her own.

When I told Jamaica we were going to have her birthday party
in two weeks, she made a face.

"Thas too far away—what if you forget or what if I not be here
anymore?"

Though I could vouch for not forgetting, I was not going to
vouch for her being in the group home. Jamaica's status was too
tenuous.

"I won't forget, Jamaica. I have a good memory and I don't
forget important things like your birthday. If you are not here on
your birthday, I promise to find you and we will have your birthday party wherever you are."

"Will you bring me my skates wherever I am?"

"Who said you were getting skates?"

"You did," Jamaica said. "You say you were gettin me skates
like Nida's mother got her, white skates with pink wheels. You
say you would ax Nida's mother where she got Nida's skates an
then you would go there an buy me my skates."

"*You* said I was getting you skates—I didn't say I was getting
you any skates. I *am* getting you a present, but I'm not telling you
what it is. I want it to be a surprise."

"Okay, but please make my surprises them pretty ol skates."

Before I left that day, Jamaica and I walked around the corner
to the bakery. She picked out her cake and we ordered it: a strawberry shortcake with creamy white frosting and red roses you
could eat. Holding my hand, Jamaica pulled me down to her
head level and whispered, "Make them put my name on it, make
them put in those words that say, 'This be the cake of Jamaica.' "

On August 28 Jamaica had her party. I had brought nine candles. It was about eleven on a hot Saturday morning when I arrived at the group home. During the previous week I had phoned
to make and get approval for our plans. First we would take the
six girls at the home out for Kentucky Fried Chicken and then
we'd go to the afternoon session at a roller-skating rink. Jamaica

held on to a few things from her past, and Kentucky Fried, as she called it, was one of them. She craved the fried chicken and mashed potatoes with gravy and biscuits that she said her mother had loved. She savored each bite, eating slowly, dreamily licking her fingers as she picked up each piece. She nibbled off the crust before she bit into the chicken. Nothing was ever thrown away. She insisted that cold mashed potatoes were good and that she could eat biscuits any time of day, and she took any leftovers home. So, with a trip to Kentucky Fried Chicken, she felt she was inviting her birthday guests to a banquet.

Jamaica opened her presents. First, a lovely gold heart necklace from Ozzie McDaniel—"I hope this be real gold and not that junk," proclaimed Jamaica. Miss Clark gave her a gospel tape of the songs they sang together. Staff gave her a baseball cap with "Jamaica" on the front.

"Well?" Jamaica looked in my direction. I gave her the package I was holding. She tore it open, all the while shouting through the restaurant, "These are my skates, I be knowin these are *my* skates." Paper, ribbon, and cardboard flew in all directions. "Yes!" she exclaimed. She immediately put on her white skates with pink wheels, and was preparing to career among the tables of Kentucky Fried Chicken when Miss Ozzie and I lifted her by the elbows and took her out to the sidewalk in front. She walked in her new skates, holding on to the fence bar by bar. Jamaica got into the car with her skates still on.

The skating party was a huge success. Everyone fell down, not just once but multiple times. The group home was strewn all over Moonglow Skating Rink. Each fall was greeted with tumbling laughter, finger-pointing, and furious attempts to lift the prone skater that ended with the rescuers' feet rolling right out from under them until they, too, were part of the pile. When Miss Ozzie McDaniel fell, the girls were so convulsed, so overcome with glee, that they all piled on top of her, covering her quite ample frame in a mass of giggling, squirming bodies.

Jamaica wanted desperately to glide, to dance with hands

crossed, and to skate backward. She held on to the side rail, walking around and around the rink, occasionally making a foray out into the middle, where she would proceed to collapse and laugh hysterically, her head thrown back, her arms propping her up. After some falls she just lay there waiting for the rink attendant to lift her. Then she held on with a death grip, her arms around his waist. It was dangerous to skate with Jamaica. Like a drowning victim, she took you down with her.

When "Happy Birthday" played on the sound system and the host invited anyone whose birthday it was to come out into the middle, receive a paper crown, and skate around the rink, several children came forward. Jamaica held tightly to the rail and hand-over-hand headed away from our group. The children called her, Miss Ozzie offered to skate with her, and one of the older girls tried to grab her and pull her into the rink.

"No way," said Jamaica. "I'm not goin out there with those fools. Besides, it's not my really birthday." She stood watching the birthday skaters go around the rink. When the song ended and all the skaters entered the rink again, Jamaica picked her way back and happily began to go around and around and to fall all over again.

Back at the group home, we put up "Happy Birthday" banners and brought out the cake. Jamaica wanted to light the candles. Everyone sang and told her to make a wish. Jamaica closed her eyes and for what seemed like a long time was quietly thoughtful. "Okay," she said, "want to know what I'm wishin for?"

"No, don't tell anyone," one of the girls instructed. "It's bad luck—then you won't ever get them."

Jamaica blew out the candles in one puff-cheeked burst. "Everyone gets a piece of them red roses," she announced. "I say so cause it be my cake."

I have a picture of Jamaica looking at her birthday cake. Her cheeks are puffed out, she is blowing out nine candles, and she is wearing her sparkly pink crown.

Chapter 10

Just as summer was ending, Miss Clark allowed Jamaica weekend visits.

The next weekend was Labor Day, and we went to the beach one more time. Though nothing had yet come of plans to remove Jamaica from the group home, there were no plans for her to start school the following week with the other girls, either. The neighborhood school did not have a program for her. Though by age Jamaica should have been in the third or fourth grade, she had spent so little time in school that she had not acquired even the rudimentary skills taught in kindergarten. So while all the other children were going off to school, Jamaica was to have home instruction until a program could be found for her—it was not clear when or where. I felt disappointed about this. I did not want her to be left behind when the others in new school clothing and backpacks full of blank notebooks set off together for school each morning.

On previous trips, Jamaica had refined her means of transport from the ferry to the house. She carried a little pillow on which she could rest her head after she situated herself across the bags and boxes in the wagon. When I suggested one day that she pull me, she answered with an unmistakable hand-on-hip, eyebrows-raised glare. She took her shoes off as soon as the ferry landed; she had memorized the combination to the lock and had the wagon waiting before Jerry and I were off the ferry. She wiggled through, squirmed around, and knocked down anyone in her path, uttering an insincere "Scuse me," which translated to all in her path as "Watch out." Verbal efforts to curtail her unbridled enthusiasm for this mission were futile. I took to waiting by the entrance to the ferry door with her, so that when the boat docked, Jamaica could be the first one off. She particularly liked to arrive after dark. She would ride atop the wagon, throw her head back on her pillow, and shine her flashlight up at the stars.

When we arrived at the house this last time, Jamaica leaped from the wagon, unlocked the door, raced in to throw her possessions into the top drawer of her bureau, then raced out again to water the garden. After she was satisfied that her tomatoes' thirst had been quenched, she filled a rubber dinghy on the deck with soapsuds, water, plastic boats, dolls, and other objects she had collected. She splashed, talked to herself, and sang at full volume for hours at a time. When it got dark, she sang louder. She invented games, tried to ride a basketball across the dinghy surface, built a bridge with an oar and tried to "tightrope"-walk. She turned plastic pails into islands and tried to get them to stay put, so that she could use them as stepping-stones. She was endlessly inventive and so content playing by herself in her dinghy that it was hard to imagine that she could ever be any trouble at all.

We were expecting a house guest on Saturday—our friend William, a man of about sixty. When I told Jamaica this, she immediately said, "That man is not sleepin in the bed wit me, no way. I don't want no smelly old man puttin his hands all over me. You get him out of my face. If that man come near my room, I be poundin on the wall hard, like this." Jamaica demonstrated violent pounding on the floor. "Then," she added, "I be kickin him like this." She demonstrated hard kicks into the air. "You better be comin quick if you be hearin my poundin. I be needin you to get him off me."

I had known it would be difficult, nearly impossible, to have Jamaica visit when anyone else was around. I knew particularly that I would have to be vigilant to the point of exhaustion if the guest was a man or young boy, because she would not leave him alone. But, because this was the last weekend I would be able to take Jamaica and I wanted to keep to the long-standing plan with our friend, I ignored all intuition and good sense. I told myself I would be able to structure things so that Jamaica would not need constant supervision and attention and I could spend some time with our friend.

I had been foolish. Now it was too late: Jamaica was here and William was on the ferry. My mind raced with possible strategies as Jamaica's powerful fantasy unfolded before me. I sat her down and told her that neither Jerry nor I would ever allow any man to touch her, that we would never allow anyone to come to our house who would want to harm her.

"In this house," I said, "men never sleep in bed with little girls. You are going to stay right in your room and have your bed all to yourself. The guest has his room and his own bed on the other side of the house."

I told Jamaica that I was sorry that men had hurt her in the past, that I knew there were those kinds of men and that she had to watch out for them, but that the men who came to this house would never touch a little girl or hurt a little girl in any way.

"Thas okay, but you still be in you room if I be needin you, right?"

I suggested we take our bikes and go to the ferry so that she could meet William. I also told her that he had children who could not come with him and that I knew he liked kids and was kind to them.

When I pointed out William at the ferry, Jamaica flew away from me faster than I could ever have imagined. She ran up to the unsuspecting man, leaped up into the air, and threw her arms around his neck, hugging him and laying her head on his shoulder. I ran after her, carried her off, and introduced her to our astonished friend. I held Jamaica's hand tightly and told her that she was not to jump on or grab the guest. I explained that just as she did not want strangers touching or grabbing her, other people did not like such behavior, either. As we were walking home, I took her aside and told her what I had told my own children years ago—that bodies are private and that William needed his body privacy, just as she needed hers. "When you don't know someone, you don't touch them. If you decide to hug someone, it is because that person is someone you know and like."

"I jus be playin," Jamaica said—the infamous words that had already caused her so much loss and trouble.

"I know," I replied. "But you cannot play by touching people and grabbing them. People don't like that. You just told me you don't want any man touching and grabbing you."

But Jamaica was all over William. She grabbed his hand when he walked down to the beach, asked him for a piggyback ride, and climbed up on his lap as he sat to watch the evening news. She completely ignored Jerry and me and became totally intent on wooing the stranger. William was astonished at this sudden and aggressive display. Though I was watching her carefully and trying to keep her distracted, at one point when I had left the room and he sat down, Jamaica was on his lap in a flash. Before he could blink an eye, much less set her down again, she was rubbing up against him in a sexually suggestive and provocative way. After that, he was wary of Jamaica and did not want her anywhere near him. He said he could envision the headlines: "Manhattan Businessman Assaults Homeless Child at House Party."

I said I'd speak to Jamaica again, telling her that she was not to climb on his lap at all and that if she wanted to sit near him, she should sit in a chair next to him. We agreed that he would say the same if she attempted to climb on his lap again. I took her for a walk and explained that William did not want anyone sitting on his lap. She could sit on my lap, or if she wanted to sit near William she could bring her chair next to his. Again I explained that body privacy is important to people and that she should not touch or grab them. Jamaica listened.

Back at the house, she sat in a chair next to William, coloring. After a while she turned to him and asked, "Do you got kids?" When William replied that he did, Jamaica asked, "Do you like them?" William said yes, he did like his kids. Jamaica nodded and went on coloring. She did not try to kiss the guest good night, nor did she need to pound on my wall.

Chapter 11

The next day the community held its annual children's race on the beach. The Peep Race is run barefoot, with the children grouped by sex and age. Jamaica would be in the eight-to-ten-year-old girls' group. When I asked her if she would like to run, she replied, "Will I win?" I told her I didn't know that, but I did know she would never win if she didn't run. I thought it might be fun, I said. I knew she was a fast runner, and if she wanted to race I would bring her. Jamaica was excited. She asked if she could practice running barefoot on the beach near our house.

When Jamaica ran, she flew. Her thin, strongly muscled legs took long strides; she held her head erect and moved her arms rhythmically and effortlessly. She was a natural athlete, a natural runner.

On the way to the race, Jamaica asked, "What if I fall?"

"If you fall, get up as quickly as you can and just keep running. Don't moan, look around, or curse," I told her. "That will all slow you down—just keep running, no matter what. And don't look around to see what the other kids are doing." As I demonstrated how that, too, could slow her down, I caught my foot on the walk and fell. This accident sent Jamaica into stomach-holding hysterics followed by a sarcastic "You better not be racin, you be comin in last."

It was a beautiful day, sunny and cool. The children milled around, some whining about being afraid to run, some demonstrating their prowess to their parents by making quick runs down the beach. Some just sat around looking quiet and scared. Jamaica walked next to me up to the registration table. She looked around and announced the obvious: "There not be bein many black kids out here—where are they?" I told her not too many black kids lived at the beach. Jamaica looked up at me and took her defiant stance: she set a hand on one hip, straightened up her small body, threw back her head, bent one knee as she thrust her foot to the side in front of her, and announced, "I'm goin to beat they white asses."

"I hope you run real fast," I replied.

Each contestant received a race T-shirt, maroon with a peep emblem and the date of the race on the front. Jamaica objected to wearing this uniform. She had saved money from running a lemonade stand at the baseball game near our house and had immediately bought herself a T-shirt with one of her favorite movie characters—Chucky, from *Child's Play*—on the front and a bloody hand on the back. Jamaica and I had had big fights in video stores over my refusal to rent the horror movies to which she was addicted. She could recite whole scripts and would often jump out to scare me with a Chucky antic when I least expected it. *Child's Play* and other horror videos had somehow made their way into the group home, where Jamaica and her housemates watched them with fascination. I didn't want to refuse to let her buy something she so desperately wanted with money she had earned. Once she owned it, she seldom wore anything else. I began to wonder if the T-shirt had become an amulet to stave off real-life horror and harm.

When Jamaica stood at the table to register, the woman asked her name and age.

"Jamaica Thomas, I'm nine," she replied.

"Where do you live, Jamaica?" the woman asked.

Jamaica was silent. "Maple and Bay Street," I answered.

"Maple and Bay Street, over there," Jamaica repeated, pointing back down the beach.

The other contestants, who were beginning to line up, all wore peep T-shirts. Jamaica announced, "I'm wearin Chucky, I'm not wearin no T-shirt with no baby chicken on it, no way."

I told Jamaica that the bird on the T-shirt was not a chicken but one of the little shorebirds that she saw darting along the water's edge, a peep. I explained that this race was named the Peep Race after the bird, because just like the bird the children ran along the beach with no shoes on. Then we tossed around the idea of a bird wearing sneakers, and Jamaica doubled over with laughter.

"Okay," she said, "I'll put on this ugly ol shirt for the race, but you hold my Chucky shirt an don't let any other kid have it. If I sees someone else wearin my Chucky shirt when I get back, I'll beat they ass."

"Don't worry, I won't let anyone touch it," I replied. Then I added, "Maybe I'll wear it myself while I wait for you—you know how much I love Chucky."

"Yeah, right." In a spirit of generosity she added, "You can if you want to, jus no one but you."

Jamaica walked across the beach to the lineup spot. "Good luck," I said. "Run as fast as you can. I'll be waiting here when you get done."

Jamaica spoke to no one. She stood alone among excited children who slapped each other on the back, wished each other luck, and gave each other high-fives. Jamaica was concentrating. She watched the race director, then stood where he told her to go. Poised for the start, she bent over slightly, one hand on her knee, the other arm behind her hip. Though no shorter than many, Jamaica was by far the thinnest child in the race. She was lean and firmly muscled, her legs without an ounce of excess fat, her peep T-shirt so large on her small body that it flapped in the wind.

When the start whistle blew, Jamaica took off down the beach in a quick, long-strided gallop. Her arms pumped rhythmically; her body was erect, head high, eyes straight ahead. Jamaica was fast. She and three other girls pulled ahead quickly. In moments they were well in front of the pack. Jamaica and two others ran in back of a taller, faster girl who inched ahead. Parents had rushed down to the turnaround point to cheer their children at the half, but I was afraid to leave the spot where I had promised to meet Jamaica, lest I get caught up in the crowd and not be able to make it back in time.

I stood alone, rooting for her. I wanted her to have the pride of accomplishment, the pleasure of winning. I also felt afraid, afraid she would fall down, drop behind, quit—somehow feel disappointment or failure. This race had been my idea; what if I had set her up? She didn't have too many emotional reserves. I hoped she could take the race as just fun, but in fact I had not seen it that way myself. I had seen it as a chance for Jamaica to accomplish something; I knew she stood a chance of doing well. I had pushed her a little, hoping she would have the pleasure of success.

"Come on, Jamaica," I said to myself. "Hang in there, keep flying."

Jamaica did just that—she pulled ahead of the other two girls in the pack and began to gain on the leader. She edged up, running faster, with no apparent fatigue. I saw the older girl glance over her shoulder; when she saw Jamaica she sped up, with Jamaica close on her heels. The older girl crossed the finish line two steps ahead. Jamaica crossed and flopped down face first on the beach, right in the path of the oncoming pack. A worried-looking race official ran over, scooped her up, and took her to the edge, where he gave her a cup of water.

"Where's Chucky?" Jamaica asked as I congratulated her on running a great race. She looked at me sideways and said, "But I didn't be winnin, less get outta here." Jamaica did not respond at all to the kids who congratulated her. She stared at them, lifted her eyebrows, tilted her head, and remained expressionless until they went away.

"Jamaica," I said, "I'm proud of you—you ran a great race, you are a good runner, and you are one of the winners." I told her there were three winners and that as the second winner she would get a medal. Avoiding what I knew could be an argument, I told her that I wanted us to stay until they gave out the medals so she could get hers, because it showed how good a runner she was and how she had learned to race today.

"Gimme Chucky," Jamaica replied. "I'm not wearin this baby chicken up to get no medal."

The older kids' race had just begun. "None of them are as fast as me," Jamaica said.

"You *are* fast, Slippery Shoes—just as fast as those little chickens."

Jamaica smiled and nodded. "I'm fast."

People cheered at the ceremony. I took a picture of Jamaica smiling at the official as she placed the long red, white, and blue ribbon with its silver peep medal around Jamaica's neck.

Back in Brooklyn, Jamaica ran up the stairs to the group home. "I won a runnin race," she announced to Staff and the other children sitting in front of the television. "I ran so fast no one could even catch me."

Staff looked up from the television and asked me, "What did she win—some Special Olympics or something?"

Before I had a chance to answer, Jamaica retorted, "Nuthin special about them races. I raced with real runnin kids, not with kids in wheelchairs—fast kids, but I'm faster."

"It was a big, big race," I said. "Forty-four kids all racing down the beach. Jamaica ran like the wind and she won this medal."

"We even had costumes that has this fast bird, the little ol peep, on it," said Jamaica as she showed the group her T-shirt.

"You done real good, Jamaica," one of the children offered.

Jamaica nodded. "I did, I really did."

We went into Jamaica's room and hung up her medal on the corner of the mirror.

Chapter 12

In the middle of the next week, I phoned the group home to talk to Jamaica and to see whether she had begun school.

"I be packin up," Jamaica announced.

"Where are you going?"

"Dunno—some new place like a school or somethin. I be leavin this place an goin there tomorrow."

"Do you know what it's called?"

"Nope—no one toll me. I jus be knowin I got to pack up, cause Staff say I be leavin this place in the mornin when the other kids be goin to school."

"Go get Staff—I want to talk to someone and find out what's happening, and don't go away, because I want to talk to you again."

A new Staff I didn't know picked up the phone.

I could feel my fear rising. "Do you know what's happening to Jamaica? She said she's packing up and leaving tomorrow. Do you know anything about the plans for her?"

Staff knew nothing—she had come on at four that afternoon and had found instructions in the daily order book to have Jamaica pack up all her belongings and be prepared to leave early in the morning. She had no idea where Jamaica was going or who was going to take her there. No one would be available with more information until Miss Clark could be contacted in the morning.

I got Jamaica back on the phone. "Jamaica, has anyone told you anything about where you are going tomorrow?"

"Unh-unh," she replied.

"Where do you think you're going?" I asked.

"Dunno," she said. "I gots to go now, Staff be lookin at me right in my face."

"Okay, listen to me. I'm going to talk to Miss Clark tomorrow. I'll find out where you are going and I'll come to visit you. I'll send you a message as soon as I know what is happening."

"Uh-huh," Jamaica replied. The phone clicked and she was gone.

All morning, between my appointments, I tried to reach Miss Clark. By the time I finally reached her, Jamaica had gone—she was no longer a resident of the group home. She had been sent upstate, to a residential school for emotionally disturbed children. Again my request to be told what was going to happen to her had been ignored. This time I was truly surprised. When Miss Ozzie had told me several weeks before that Jamaica was not fitting in at the group home and therefore was unlikely to stay, I immediately went to Miss Clark to request that she let me know of any plans to move Jamaica to another placement. Miss Clark had been friendly—she seemed to like Jamaica, to wish her well, and to understand that it might be useful if I accompanied Jamaica to her new residence to help her get settled and to make plans to visit soon.

"When I learned yesterday that Jamaica was going to leave and that she had to be taken to her new placement by a Bureau of Child Welfare worker," Miss Clark said, "I thought there was no use in calling you because you wouldn't be permitted to take her there. I planned to let you know today that she was gone and where she's at."

I could see Miss Clark's goodwill, but it was hard to under-

stand why no one seemed to grasp the importance of Jamaica
having someone she knew with her when she was sent away to an
unknown place. If I was not going to be permitted to accompany
the Bureau of Child Welfare worker, I wondered why Miss Clark
had not gone. Jamaica had been sent away from her precarious
home, with a strange man she had never seen, to begin life in a
totally foreign place once again. It seemed impossible to per-
suade anyone of the importance of watching over her. Some time
ago I had begun to suspect that it was more than Jamaica's tough-
ness, more than her difficult personality, that prevented her care-
takers from feeling kindly and protective toward her. I felt that it
was Jamaica's very situation, the circumstances of her abject life,
her total aloneness that had debased her in the eyes of others. It
was as though the fact that she was not loved made her unlov-
able; that no mother cared about her seemed to invite callous
disregard. Everything that had been done to her somehow
seemed to make her unworthy of tenderness. Jamaica had been
marked as untouchable; people did not identify with her or feel
compassion for her. I couldn't imagine that what had just happened to her would ever have happened to Luz and Nida.

Miss Clark told me not to feel bad and asked whether, now
that Jamaica had been sent upstate, I would like to be a Big Sister to one of the other girls in the group home. I told her I
planned to stick with Jamaica. There was the silence of nothing
more to say. I found out the name of the institution and hung up.

IT WAS THE end of September before I saw Jamaica again.
Until then she seemed to have vanished once more. Hilltop, the
school upstate, did not allow a child to receive phone calls unless
they were placed to the office of the child's social worker. But no
social worker was assigned to Jamaica, so she could not be
phoned. After several frustrated calls to Hilltop's social service
department and many unkept promises by social workers to find
out which of Hilltop's cottages Jamaica was living in and whom

I could contact to make plans to speak with and visit her, I phoned the office of the school's director and left a message threatening to go to the Bureau of Child Welfare with my concerns about how a child I believed to be in their custody had been lost. The director returned my call within the hour.

"Miss Hayes," I said to the crisp, foreign-accented voice on the other end of the line, "I'm furious! I have been trying to get in touch with a homeless child who I know was moved to your facility from a group home in Brooklyn two weeks ago. I've called at least twenty times, but no one ever returns my calls. For all I know, or the world knows, this child may never have arrived at Hilltop School. I want to know if she is there, and I want to talk to her. If I can't, I want to know why."

Within an hour, Jamaica phoned me from the office of Miss Jones, a social worker.

"This is Linda. How are you?"

"Okay."

"I've been trying to get in touch with you since you left the group home, but it was hard to get someone to take you to her office so I could call you or you could call me."

"Uh-huh."

"Are you living with other girls in a cottage?"

"Uh-huh."

"What is the cottage called?"

"Building Twenty."

"What are you doing there?"

"Nuthin."

"Are you going to school?"

"Uh-huh."

"Do you like it?"

"Uh-huh."

I could hear rustling in the background, a whispered message that time was up. I would get no further than the disembodied "uh-huh"; there would be no elaboration, no news or stories to tell.

"I'll be up to see you this coming weekend, either Saturday or Sunday—whichever day they will let visitors come. Put Miss Jones back on so that I can make the plans with her."

I asked Miss Jones about the rules. She said I could visit for one hour on Sunday. I would not be allowed to take Jamaica "off grounds" until Hilltop had checked out my volunteer status. She spun a web of red tape: this would take some time; she could not say how long; someone would look into it and call me back. She did not mention the forms I knew I would need to fill out. "Who has the forms I need, how will I get them?" I asked.

"She's not here today," Miss Jones replied.

"Will she be there on Sunday? Is anyone there to talk to visitors on Sunday?"

"Someone is here."

"Who?"

"The Staff on weekend."

"Who will that be? Is there a schedule up so that I can call and make sure she has the forms I need?"

"I don't know."

"Can you go find out, or can I call someone?"

A labored sigh fogged the phone line. Silence was followed by drawers slamming and a rattling of papers.

"I'm on."

To ask Miss Jones for her extension would be a declaration of war. I could sense I had already asked her to exert herself far beyond what she felt was fair or reasonable. She wanted me to go away, or, as she probably would have put it, to get out of her face. Talking to Miss Jones was like talking to a withholding child in the midst of a temper tantrum.

In the many years since I had worked with and been trained and taught by Annie Lees, a child therapist at the Jewish Board of Guardians, I had often recalled and followed her teaching and example. Her wisdom had stood me in good stead, useful far beyond its application to therapeutic work with children. When I first met Annie she was an eighty-year-old woman talking brightly and continuously to a sullen three-year-old boy who had just wreaked havoc on the snack table of the play therapy room. He was standing with his back to her, immovable with rage. Annie was going over the incident, telling the story as it had happened, crash by damning crash, recalling and retelling the unpleasant incident in detail. There was no accusation, no reference to the boy or to why he'd thrown all the snacks on the floor. There was no direct confrontation. The child was silent. Annie chattered on.

"I call it cocktail-party conversation for children," she told me later, in her soft German accent. "Sometimes it is too soon; the ground is not fertile to address the hostility directly. You have to make the atmosphere lighter—not forget, but wait for your moment. Nothing else is possible. If you do otherwise, you make matters much worse."

So I chattered at Miss Jones's passive-aggressive silence and hostility: "Okay, thanks a lot. I'll see you on Sunday so that you can give me the forms; that will hurry things along. I know it might take a few weeks to get volunteer status at Hilltop. Please tell Jamaica I will visit her for one hour on Sunday. I know I can't take her off grounds, but please let her know I will bring a picnic."

Jamaica was drifting and whirling in a system that had no real interest in or hold on her. She was shuffled hither and yon, wherever a slot might open. This time the winds had blown her north—upstate to Hilltop. And even before I had met anyone at this new place, my interest in Jamaica was again an annoyance to the people in charge—the very people whose help I needed. Yet Jamaica had not vanished. One gesture still remained feasible: I could show up for one hour, and I could bring Kentucky Fried.

Chapter 13

It was a chilly gray Sunday afternoon when I pulled up into the circular driveway in front of a four-story redbrick building that looked as though it had once been an elegant Victorian mansion. Huge old oak trees were turning color on the front lawn. Black wrought-iron balconies hung in front of the French windows on the second and third floors. Fireplace chimneys lined the roof. The beauty of the building was in sharp contrast to the deteriorated wooden sign, "Administration," stenciled in black letters on a white board and stuck in the ground of the front lawn. Not a person was in sight. I headed up long wide steps and found the door unlocked, so I walked into the lobby. A circular staircase led to the floor above. The building appeared deserted. I listened for some sign of life and eventually heard footsteps directly overhead.

"Anybody here?" I shouted up the empty staircase.

When after two more tries there was still no response, I made my way up the staircase, headed toward the noise, and knocked at the window of an office door labeled "Social Service." Through the glass, I saw coming toward me the top of a head adorned with gold, red, and green beads woven into an abundance of small neat braids. A black woman dressed in a pink running suit opened the door. She appeared to be about twenty-five.

"Are you Miss Jones?" I inquired.

"No," she replied in a deep southern accent. "She's not on today. I'm Miss Higby."

When I told her who I was, she invited me in. I followed her down an aisle lined with stored oak office desks and chairs to the back of the room, where a teenage girl sat on a stool beside Miss Higby's desk. Combs, colored beads, and hair lotions had been laid out on the desk, which was serving as a dressing table for Miss Higby's work on the girl's hair. A small television was tuned to football.

"You a football fan?" Miss Higby asked.

"Not football—I don't understand it—but baseball and also basketball."

She watched the TV intently for a moment before turning to me. "I just got Jamaica's case. I don't know much about her yet."

"No one knows much about her," I said. "I was told she was picked up one day on her own in the Port Authority. No one connected to her has ever been found." I told Miss Higby what little I had been told about Jamaica, filling her in on recent history. She listened while periodically glancing at the TV and assuring the child whose hair she was beading that she would finish the job soon. I told Miss Higby that I would like to continue my volunteer relationship with Jamaica and asked whether there was a program here, as there had been at Mercy, that I could work through.

"There should be, but there isn't," she replied. "We don't have anything like that right now, though we do have volunteers that come into the school to read to the kids, teach them crafts or sports. But it's not like a Big Sister or Big Brother program. Too bad, too, as you can see our kids don't get many visitors. Today is a visiting day and there is barely anyone here. Tisha here is waiting for her aunt to come. She has been waiting in my office since one, and now it's three. We've been calling, but no answer. Don't look like anyone is visiting you today, Tisha—right?"

Tisha was silently lining up the beads by color on the desk.

"That's okay, Tisha," Miss Higby went on. "We'll make you beautiful for those mean little boys out there. These kids are used to it," she said to me, as though the child were not in the room.

Miss Higby gave me the forms and told me that I should send them back to her. She would have them processed so I could take Jamaica off grounds for the day. Eventually, if I wanted her, she could visit at home for weekends. When I said that this was exactly what I wanted, Miss Higby offered the information that Hilltop had a van that took kids into the city and dropped them off at the home they were visiting. Usually, she went on to say, the children taking the van were being returned to their homes or being sent to foster homes for weekend trial visits; she wasn't sure van service could be arranged for Jamaica to visit me.

We walked to the west end of the long office room and looked out the window onto the two streets of cottages behind the building. This was the girls' area of the campus. The cottages were arranged according to age groups; the youngest girls were five, the oldest seventeen. The youngest lived closest to the school itself, a long, modern two-story building of red brick, next to Administration. The oldest lived farthest away, in the last cottage on the second street back. Building Twenty—Miss Higby pointed it out—was the second building on the second street. All the cottages were identical, low, one-story yellow-brick buildings. There were no trees along the streets, no bushes or landscaping around the cottages. Paths around the cottages were worn into dusty ruts. Some cottages had clotheslines strung across the backyards; some had redwood picnic benches. There was so little to distinguish one cottage from the other, I thought it must be very difficult for new children to find their way around.

"How many kids live here?"

"We can take anywhere up to two hundred and fifty. Right now we are really high—maybe even over two hundred and fifty. Crack has been boosting up our numbers."

In the playground next to the school, a young woman turned a tire swing around and around until the chain holding it was wound tight. She stepped back and let the swing spin, to the delight of the little boy waving from inside the circle. Again and again she wound and he spun. Miss Higby joined me at the window. We watched the young woman take the little boy from the swing and walk to a bench, where she sat him on her lap. She took some food from her knapsack, set out a piece of newspaper between them, and spat on a napkin to wash his hands. They began to eat their picnic.

"I know I can only stay an hour."

"No one really cares how long you stay. Just ask cottage Staff what time they're going to eat. They don't like to have kids late—they have to feed them, clean up, and get things over with."

Miss Higby had been friendly and helpful. I thanked her and on the way out asked, "If things go well for Jamaica here, is it likely that this will be her home through high school?"

Miss Higby looked surprised. She shook her head. "We try never to keep children past two years—what we aim for is return home if there is a home, and if not, foster placement, group home, or, best of all, adoption. Jamaica has no relatives, so adoption might be an option if she is not too disturbed. Nine-year-old disturbed kids are impossible to place. Do you want her?"

Miss Higby's words gave form to my troubling thoughts. Where was Jamaica going to live? What was going to be her home? Who would care for her? When I learned she was going to Hilltop, I had felt a measure of relief. I knew Hilltop to be a residential treatment center with a school that ran from first grade through twelfth. I thought this might be just right for

Jamaica—she could settle in, make a place for herself, be cared for, and begin to get the psychological treatment and the education she so desperately needed. This grim news took me aback. I had never suspected that Hilltop was another interim placement, that Jamaica had come here only to wait to be moved again.

In the absence of a permanent home, someone to belong to, Jamaica was beginning to belong to me. I was becoming more than I had wanted to be or ever dreamed of being to her: the only constant in her life. I had to rethink what I was doing and what I might try to do.

I headed back to the car and drove very slowly toward Building Twenty. A group of teenage girls sat together on a wall in back of the administration building. They looked up and watched me pass before handing around a cigarette, which I caught sight of in my rearview mirror.

Hilltop reminded me of the residential treatment school where I had worked nearly twenty years before. Some of the features were the same: the huge campus with ball fields and a playground, the big brick administration building and school, the children milling around, the small clusters of adolescents standing around outside to sneak a smoke. On Sundays it was as stark and quiet as Hilltop was. Desolation seemed to creep out of the buildings and empty into the streets. Most children had little to do on Sundays. Those with visitors sat and talked around tables; the others waited for the visitors to leave, so that they could stop being reminded of who had not come to see them.

I thought of Lanie and her daughter and remembered that Lanie was just about Jamaica's age when I saw her for the last time as a child. Lanie would not be pushing her child on a tire swing, like the mother I had just seen from the window. I doubted that the Catwoman had ever come up on the van from the city. Probably Lanie, like Tisha, had waited and waited. Lanie had stayed at her residential school through twelfth grade. Things had changed drastically since that time, when each cottage had house parents, a "Mom and Pop" who lived there full-time, and when it was not unusual for some children to remain until they went off to college or a job. Some left to live in apartments run by the same agency that ran the school. This was what I'd had in mind for Jamaica. I now knew I could not hope for it.

I parked the car in a vacant lot near Building Twenty and headed over. When no one answered my knock, I opened the door and walked inside. Entering the building was like stepping into a tunnel. The front door opened into one huge room. It took a moment for my eyes to get accustomed to the lack of light. The farther into the room you went, the darker it was, although dim light seeped in around the edges of the room from behind thick orange curtains. Children and Staff were sitting toward the back of the room on couches, on chairs, and in small bunches grouped together on the floor around the television set, which lit up the space directly around it so that some faces were visible. I could not recognize Jamaica in the huddle of children and Staff wrapped up in blankets and bedspreads. I was suddenly the center of attention.

"Who she is?" a child asked Staff before I'd had a chance to introduce myself.

At last I spotted Jamaica in the corner, looking in my direction with no more sign of recognition or greeting than she'd have granted a complete stranger. This lack of recognition did not seem to bother Staff or make her wonder whether Jamaica really knew me. Staff looked around and found Jamaica's head sticking up out of a bedspread the same color and pattern as the curtains.

"Come here, child," Staff said in a strong West Indian accent.

Jamaica moved slowly in my direction. She responded to my greeting with her characteristic hand-on-hip, head-tilted glare.

"Did you wonder what happened to me?" I asked as we left the cottage and headed down the parking lot toward the car.

Jamaica shook her head no. She shrugged her shoulders and raced off toward the car. She went to the driver's side, opened the door, got in, held the wheel, and pretended to drive. I got in on the other side, sat in the passenger seat, and asked, "Where are you taking us?"

"Out of this fuckin dump, back to my house on a Hundred an Thirty-fifth Street," she said. "An I be doin the drivin."

"How about eating our Kentucky Fried before we take off?"

"You bring it?"

"Follow your nose."

Jamaica peered around the seat into the back of the car. When she spotted the Colonel gazing at her from the bag on the backseat, she shouted "Yes!," leaped over the seat, and began to set out her feast.

"We can go outside and make a picnic if you want."

"Not me—I'm stayin right in my cozy ol car and eatin me some Kentucky Fried with biscuits, mashed, and gravy."

Jamaica was silent as she ate. She took pieces of skin off the chicken and broke the pieces into smaller pieces, which she put in a pile and ate one by one. She did not mix the gravy and potatoes; she dipped her spoon into the gravy, scooped up a small bit, then gingerly added a tiny scoop of potatoes. She licked her bony fingers and greased her face as she wiped around her mouth and concentrated her full attention on her meal. When she finished eating, she said, "Okay, less go to you house. I needs to get some of my stuff from the piano chair." I told her we could not go for a few weeks yet, until they checked me out and gave me permission to take her home. Jamaica said, "Thas stupid, cause I be knowin you for a long time now, nearly my whole life."

Jamaica did not want to take a walk around the school and show it to me, as I suggested; she wanted to stay in the car, where it was warm, and drive around. She sat on my lap, turning the wheel with me as we drove slowly up and down the streets, to the front gate and back, down the hill to the end of the school property, up the hill to the other end. We came back to the beginning and started our route all over.

"You bring me my tapes from you house?" Jamaica asked.

I handed her the blue plastic box that held her four or five favorites. She looked through it, recognized the picture on the one she wanted, took it out, put it into the player and turned the volume up.

We drove around and around the campus, Bob Marley and Jamaica singing together at top volume the lyrics from her favorite reggae song—"Don't worry bout a thing, cause every little thing is gonna be all right."

Chapter 14

When I arrived on visiting day two weeks later, Jamaica was expecting me. Miss Higby had told her I was coming. It was a warm Indian summer afternoon. Staff had put a kitchen chair outside the door, where she sat watching the girls jump rope. Four or five ropes were swinging as children jumped and chanted rhythmic counting songs—"How many candies for your best sweetheart, one two, three . . ."

"I be learnin double Dutch," Jamaica said. "Watch me go." She stood in line behind three other little girls while two girls swung two ropes. The jumper had to have perfect timing to jump in and clear both ropes at once. Once cleared, she moved in time from side to side, jumping each rope in turn. If the jumper made it in and began to jump, the children all began the well-known chants. There was a ritual to getting in. The child stood watching the ropes, waiting for just the right moment, her head moving from side to side, her arms outstretched in front, palms facing the ropes. She moved her arms back and forth rhythmically, a pendulum indicating the tempo and helping her find the balance needed to jump. Most jump-ins ended with a foot caught in a rope. The swinging stopped. Each jumper got three tries, then went to the end of the line. If you succeeded in jumping, it became your turn to swing the ropes.

Jamaica stood in front of the ropes, assumed the entry position, moved her hands rhythmically back and forth, her skinny body taut, poised, ready to spring at exactly the right moment to clear the ropes and be set for the first jump. She made it in on the first try and jumped continuously through a whole song—"Sally had a baby, named him Sunny Jim, put him in the bathtub to teach him how to swim. Drank all the water, ate all the soap, died last night with a bubble in his throat. In came the doctor, in came the nurse, in came the lady with the big fat purse." Jamaica was firm with concentration. She went on to the second song, springing up lightly with each jump, her feet landing so smoothly she barely raised a puff of dust around her ankles. Suddenly, for no apparent reason, Jamaica just quit. In characteristic fashion she tired abruptly of the activity, flung herself on the ground on top of the ropes, and started laughing and rolling. When she would not get up, the other girls started yelling at her: if she didn't want to keep on jumping, it was her turn to swing the ropes. Jamaica rolled off the ropes and stood up, but would not take the ropes' end to swing.

Cries of "That's not fair!" followed her as she walked away from the game. "If you be jumpin you got to be swingin," one of the girls shouted at her. The agreement was struck: unless Jamaica came back to swing, she wouldn't be allowed to play again. Jamaica kept walking down the street, toward the playground. Staff yelled after her to get back and swing or she would not be permitted a visit with me. I would be sent home. "If you can't act right you are not fit for company," Staff told her with certainty.

Jamaica stood alone in the middle of the road. She glared at the group of girls, her face solemn and immobile. Slowly, without a word, looking past all the children, she walked back, took up the ropes, and began to try to swing. After a moment or two it was apparent that she could not get the rhythm or the coordi-

nation necessary to keep both ropes moving in opposite directions at the same pace. She jerked the rope out of the other girl's
hand, twisted one rope in the other, made the ropes clash in
midair and sent them swinging the wrong way. The jumper
found no steady motion or rhythm to fix on; she could not jump
in and the game stopped. Jamaica threw down the ropes and
walked away again. This time Staff said nothing. Another girl
picked up the ropes and began to swing; the game went on without Jamaica.

I caught up with her as she made her way toward the car in the
parking lot.

"You got food?" she asked. "Kentucky Fried? I wuz gonna ax
you if my fren Tanika could have some food and walk around wit
us. I promise her I think she could, but now she be all mad at me
an everything. I toll her she could have some of my Kentucky
Fried and my candy that you wuz bringin."

"Maybe she won't stay mad when she hears about Kentucky
Fried. Let's go ask her and Staff if she can walk around with us."

Jamaica pointed out Tanika, who stared at us from the sidelines of the double Dutch game. She was a tall child, dark in
complexion, dressed in short shorts with basketball socks pulled
nearly up to her knees. When she spoke, I could see she was
missing several lower front teeth. Jamaica cupped her hand
around Tanika's ear and whispered. Tanika smiled and nodded.

Staff said Tanika could join us to walk around—but, she cau-
tioned me, "Those two are the worst in the cottage—always bad,
never doing right. You have to watch out for them. They'll be up
to something." I wished Staff wouldn't talk about Jamaica this
way when she was present and could hear. It seemed that whenever I was with her, the other adults in her life had nothing good
to say, and they always said their nothing good right in front of
her. Feeling I had to defend her, yet not wanting to alienate
someone who could make her life worse, I replied in words that
Jamaica passed on to me from Miss Pope—words that I knew
meant affection to her: "Sometimes this bad little girl can really

get herself messed up, but most of the time she's pretty good. I have a lot of fun with her."

"Well, you be good today," Staff admonished, adding the condescending threat I loathed and that made me cringe each of the many times Staff in all Jamaica's temporary homes used it: "—or this lady won't be bothering with you anymore." Jamaica did not react to this. "Less go," she said, dragging Tanika by the hand.

The girls walked ahead of me, whispering conspiratorially, glancing back at me now and then to see if I could overhear. Then Jamaica turned back and announced, "Tanika and me got somethin to show you, and it's scary. Less eat first, then we take you to our scary place."

We spread out the picnic cloth I had brought. Jamaica took charge and began to divide the chicken in her usual fashion, tearing the skin off first, then tearing the meat off the bones with her fingers and licking her fingers frequently as she worked. Tanika objected: "Don't touch my chicken like that. Jus gimme my piece. I don't want you dirty hands that been touchin you booty messin up my nice chicken."

Jamaica threw back her head and laughed. She poked around in the chicken and finally pointed out a piece Tanika could take. "You be wantin any, Auntie?" she asked, using a name for me that I had not heard before.

Tanika looked at Jamaica and asked, "She be you aunt? Not you really aunt, can't be cuz she be white white and we be black."

"She my really aunt," Jamaica responded. "She not be white anyway, she jus look white. She be what my grandma say is light-skinned. She look like me."

Tanika looked at me with disbelief. Neither she nor Jamaica said any more about my "auntie" status or my skin color. They went on eating until there was not a trace of food left. Even the crispy crumbs had been picked off the cloth.

"Now for some Chucky," Jamaica announced, rolling her eyes and making scary sounds.

Jamaica said some boys in her school had sneaked away at recess, taking her and Tanika with them to show them something in the woods. "We would be in big, big trouble if Staff see us, but we snuck off and snuck back wit no one seein us." We walked the length of campus to a small, abandoned brick caretaker's cottage. A path led into the woods from an old rock garden at the side of the cottage.

Jamaica led the way. Tanika kept dropping back until she was nearly walking beside me. We walked along the path into a clearing where a small, weathered picket fence surrounded a stone on which a bronze plaque had been placed.

"Read it to me, Auntie," Jamaica asked, holding my hand in a firm grip as she looked expectantly at the stone.

The plaque read:

LADY DAY
1950–1966
This small cat was the beloved
friend of many children.

I wondered who had been the Billie Holiday fan and whether he or she had played her songs for the children.

Jamaica's eyes widened. "Less get us outta here." She looked all around, and Tanika started to cry.

"She be cryin cuz boys tell us that the ghostis of the cat stay up in those trees, an if you don't watch youself, the ghostis jump down on you, rip out you eyes, eat up you skin, an scratch you so bad that all you blood run out you body an you jus lay here dead till the animals in these woods eat you all up. Kids be disappearin like that before, an no one ever seen them anymore, not even they bones."

Although frightened, Jamaica was also very excitedly telling her story to scare Tanika, me, and herself. Tanika was stiff with fear, holding me tightly, shivering.

"Those boys were trying to scare you—there are no cat ghosts in the trees. They were making up a story to get you frightened."

I said I thought that Lady Day must have been a very sweet cat whom children loved and who loved children. "That's why they made such a special place to bury her. But," I added, aware that Jamaica might be headed for trouble if she continued to sneak away from school to go with boys into the woods, "it isn't a good idea to come into the woods alone. Something could happen to you and no one would know where you were."

"Staff tell us to stay out the woods too. Did you hear of that group Kew Klus Klan? They be white people who look for black people to kill. Staff say a kid went in the woods by mistake, a man Kew Klus Klan got her, slit her throat, an put her out on the steps of the cottage. Lots of white people up here don't like kids in the school cuz mostly we be black."

Tanika added that Staff told them last week that she had seen one of the Kew Klus Klan walking around the cottage and that if the girls saw any white people walking around at night it was likely the Kew Klus Klan coming to kill them.

"You know about them white people?" Jamaica asked as we left the woods and walked back down the road toward the cottage. The sun was beginning to set; all the children were back inside. It was time to leave.

I was disheartened to realize that Staff was telling tall tales of horror and bigotry, making up their own versions of horror movies, instilling and inflaming racial fear in an attempt to control these vulnerable children. And if this was going on, it probably extended far past one story about the Klan, so what I might be able to do to counteract this racial propaganda wasn't likely to have much impact on these frightened little girls. Still, they had trusted me with their fears, and I wanted to try to do something to ease them. I felt the best weapon against these lies was to tell the children the truth.

The girls were attentive as we walked along and I told them, "There was a group of bad white people called the Ku Klux Klan. They lived far away from here, not even in New York. They were very bad people. Lots of good white and black people knew how bad those Ku Klux Klan were, so they got together, punished them, and made them stop hurting black people. They never lived here." I added, "They were never around the cottage or the school. Let's ask Staff to see why someone said that scary thing to you."

"She say they be no Kew Klus Klan," Jamaica announced to Staff as soon as we walked in the door. "She say they never live here, they never be round the school."

Jamaica and Tanika stood at my side, each holding a hand, listening intently as I spoke. "These kids are frightened that there are white people, Ku Klux Klan, walking around at night waiting to kill them," I told Staff. "I told them that it isn't true, that there are no Ku Klux Klan around here, that they never lived near here and they never will. I told them that they do not have to be afraid at night, that no one is hiding in the woods waiting to kill them, and that no Ku Klux Klan has ever killed or hurt a child at this school."

Staff laughed. "We just say that so that they won't go wandering around out in the woods. Something has to make them afraid. Most of the kids, especially these two, aren't afraid of anything."

"These two are terrified," I answered. "They are not about to go out into the woods at night, but I still think it is important for them to know that there is no one out in the woods waiting to kill or harm them, and, if they see a white person walking around the cottage, they don't have to be afraid."

I had no doubt of the depth of Tanika's and Jamaica's fear, and it seemed certain that with no family and friends to hold them safe and protect them, they had many more real dangers to face than the Ku Klux Klan or the ghostis of Lady Day.

Chapter 15

A week before Halloween my phone rang.

"Is me, Auntie," the husky voice on the other end of the line announced. "Staff say I can call you an tell you to git up here an help me wit my Halloween costume. I tell Staff you take me to you house an we go shoppin in you neighborhood. You know that maskis store we used to look in sometimes? We can get me a real scary maskis there."

"I wish I could—I would love to get a scary mask for that face of yours. But I am not planning to visit you until next weekend, when you're coming home with me to stay overnight. That's going to be the day after Halloween. What I can do is to go to the store, buy a mask, and send it up to you. Describe to me what you want."

"You be wrong—Staff say you have to come to get me and I have to go wit you to you house. Here, talk wit Miss Higby—she tell you."

Miss Higby got on the phone. "Miss Atkins, Jamaica wanted to call you to see if she could go to your house for a day. I told her you weren't coming up again until next Friday. Jamaica insisted that you would help her with her Halloween costume—that you have lots of dress-up clothes she can wear. She has been pestering me all morning, running in and out of my office—finally I gave in and let her call."

Miss Higby had been very helpful. When no one answered her requests about my volunteer status, she put pressure on Mercy until the information was sent. She thought that Jamaica should be permitted these visits with me, and she did everything in her power to expedite them. Miss Higby explained that until she took this job three months ago, she had been an Army recruiter. She was, she said, used to finding her way through red tape when she wanted to expedite her goals.

"This child needs a change of scenery," she said when she first called to tell me she had secured the necessary permission. "You can take her for one-day visits on either Saturdays or Sundays from noon until suppertime at six, and you can take her for weekends from after school at three on Friday until suppertime at six on Sunday. She can visit as often as you want her. When I told Jamaica this news," Miss Higby went on, "she jumped up, wrapped her legs around my waist, and nearly squeezed the breath out of me. This bad child is all packed and ready to leave this minute."

Now, Miss Higby was talking partly to me and partly to Jamaica, who was grabbing the phone and starting a tussle. "Jamaica, sit down and wait until I'm through talking or you won't be going anywhere."

I told Miss Higby that although I had not planned to come up again until next weekend, I knew how important Halloween was to Jamaica. I would try to arrange things to come up on Sunday, when I could take her for the afternoon.

"It's okay if you can't," Miss Higby replied. "She can't always get her way, but she was so determined this time, I thought I'd let her try." She asked that I come to her office to sign papers and write down what we were going to do and the hours Jamaica would be away.

"You be on time," Jamaica admonished me. "I be gettin my booty outta here."

Miss Higby laughed and murmured, "Jamaica, watch your language," in a tone that indicated both humor and, I hoped, real affection. This was the first time any Staff had taken the initiative to do something helpful for Jamaica.

ON SUNDAY, JAMAICA was sitting with her coat on. When she saw me she ran out of the cottage and without waiting for me headed straight for the car, opened the door on the driver's side, and got in. I thought I should let Staff see I had actually arrived and taken her, so I went into the cottage and found my way through the children watching TV over to Staff, who was sitting by herself in a corner knitting. Before I had a chance to say anything, she looked at me and said, "All right." I turned and walked back through the darkened room past the children. Just as I got to the door I heard a voice from the group say, "Bye, Miss Auntie."

I looked back and returned the greeting. "Bye, Tanika." I was glad to leave the darkened room and return to the fall sunshine. Jamaica was sitting in the driver's seat. She turned the wheel furiously. She talked a mile a minute to herself as she moved her head from side to side, speeded up hills, screeched around corners, and shouted at people to move over or she would run them down.

"I be drivin to you house. Less go—we gotta get outta here. We don't have much time to get my costume."

"We have to stop at Miss Higby's office to sign you out."

Jamaica sat on my lap turning the wheel on the slow drive to the administration building. "We not stoppin—less jus go. Miss Higby be knowin I'm wit you."

"We have to stop. You have to go in with me, because if we don't obey the rules, everyone will get mad at us, and then they could say they won't let you come anymore. We don't want that."

Jamaica was in Miss Higby's office by the time I was opening the front door.

"I sign you name for us—Miss Higby say that be fine, so less go."

I knew that Jamaica could neither read nor write, so I continued on to the office. Miss Higby shook her head and laughed as she handed me a form that had a huge scribble on it. I signed my name over the scribble and joined Jamaica back in the car, where she was setting up her Bob Marley tape.

"Don't worry bout a thing, cause every little thing gonna be all right" blasted from the windows Jamaica had rolled down to spread the good news in reggae duet throughout the campus. We drove down the road past the cottages where children sat on the steps talking, staring at us silently, or walking across the lawn alone to unknown destinations. Jamaica did not look right or left; her head was thrown back, her eyes closed, and she sang to the ceiling, moving in slow dance rhythm beneath her seat belt.

"Auntie, tell me when we're outta here, tell me when we git by those stone things and are on the big road—thas when I be openin my eyes."

We continued our fifteen-mile-per-hour crawl up the hill, past the school, past the empty baseball diamond and the swimming pool closed for the winter, past the spot where Jamaica had taken me to Lady Day's grave. A slight breeze wandered between me and Jamaica, a pleasant breeze, soothing and welcome. For a few moments, as Jamaica sang and I drove, it appeared that every little thing might stand a chance.

Somewhere on the parkway, as we drove through the orange and red glow of changing leaves, Jamaica announced that something had happened last night, something good and bad. When it happened she had been asleep. Jamaica told me her dream.

"I be wit my mother again. I be sittin on her lap an she be pattin my hair. We have got us a house, one of those kinds you see on TV wit that spiky kind of fence all around. That fence keep everyone bad out but keep my mother an me in, an we have a TV we watchin an a little dog like the one I had once. I brung him in, but someone killed him, beat him wit a big stick, an he be all quiet and stuff—blood comin outta he mouth. This little dog just sittin wit me an my mother while we talkin. I feel happy, it seem like it be real, my mother look like my really mother an the dog like the really dog an thas it. I wish I be in that house with my mother an that little ol dog."

We were quiet for a while. I felt Jamaica's longing. She changed the tape and mood to sensual with Madonna's "Like a Prayer." Then she turned to me. "Could you drive me by my ol house? I know it be on a Hundred an Thirty-fifth Street. We could jus drive by an look around—maybe I be seein my mother. Sometimes she be hangin out on one of those corners wit mens an stuff. I could tell her where I wuz, and then she would come an get me."

Immediately I felt afraid. When Jamaica told me her dream, I too wished she could see her mother, and now I wondered if in fact she might be found on 135th Street. Still, I didn't want to drive through central Harlem. I thought it could be dangerous: Jamaica had very little self-control, and I was nearly certain that if she did see her mother, she would bolt from the car. In her situation, that's what I would have done. I pictured Jamaica in her dream, sitting in a pretty house, petting the dog who had been killed, and once again seeing the face of her "really mother"— the mother she longed for—before sleep ended and with its ending stole her mother once again from sight and touch.

Jamaica's mother was completely lost to her. Not only could she not find Bunny, but she feared Bunny could never find her. I was curious about 135th Street. Jamaica talked about it over and over again. It seemed to be the only real place Jamaica remembered, the only place she'd been with her mother that held some security. I wanted to see it with her, to go over her past there, and if possible take down the name and address of the West Indian grocery store in hopes that Miss Higby might contact the grocer and come up with a lead. I felt Miss Higby might try. With

Jamaica, I began to think that the drive across 135th Street could hold promise. At the same time, I did not want to put either myself or Jamaica in danger.

"If you want to go back to your old neighborhood and look around as we drive by, that's okay," I said finally. "I'll drive you by there. But you have to promise me one thing that might be hard for you to do: you have to promise me that if we see your mother, you won't leap out of the car and go running in the street trying to get to her. I think that promise might be very, very hard for you to keep. I know how much you want your mother, and I understand that—I would too. But, if we go, you absolutely have to stay right in the car, even if we do see her, because if you saw her and ran out of the car, it could be very, very dangerous for both of us."

But I began to have second thoughts. I fantasized a horrible situation in which Jamaica saw her mother, leaped out of the car in the middle of 135th Street, and ran off. Then, I would have to abandon the car in the middle of the street and race down the block after her—only, in my fantasy, to have her disappear into the streets, which would close up to take her back. Jamaica liked the streets—she longed to be back there. She might try to stay on 135th Street with or without her mother.

Jamaica was uncharacteristically quiet. She looked out the window at the Hudson as Madonna sang on. Finally she turned to me, tilted her head, and in a more somber voice than I had ever heard her use said, "Less not go—less go to you house an get my maskis. I be knowin somethin. If I see my mother, I git out of this car so fass you never catch me. When you come runnin up after me to git me an my mother see you, she kill you. She jus take out her knife an stab you in you heart. My mother hate all white people. She say they always be in her face, tellin her to do this wit me or do that wit me. When she see you wit me, she just be so mad an mean, you can't fight her an you be dead. Less jus go git my maskis."

As Jamaica reasoned why we should not go to 135th Street, I was struck by the memory of one of my professors at the Child Development Center. This professor, a Jewish refugee, had fled the Holocaust to London, where he lived and worked for a long time. He told me of a fine spring day in the late 1940s when he was just beginning his career as a psychologist. That afternoon, he was hiking in the countryside with a group of young boys who had been relocated to England by the charity organization for which he worked. All the children in the group home where he was a house father had been brought there directly from newly liberated concentration camps. In my professor's group home and others, efforts were made to strengthen the children and to salvage their ravaged minds and bodies.

One boy of ten was particularly troubled. He had stopped speaking and was frequently hostile, aggressive, and destructive toward other children. The consensus among the professional staff was that he was attached to no one. It was felt that the destruction of his entire family had been so devastating that his prospects of any decent recovery were grim.

As the group hiked along through the countryside, they saw a farmer walking across the fields toward them. He was accompanied by a large German shepherd, which bounded ahead. As the farmer approached, the dog ran toward the group and headed for the professor, who, in greeting, held out his hand for the dog to sniff. When the young boy saw the German shepherd approach the professor, his face distorted with panic. He screamed out, ran over to his house father, and with all his ten-year-old strength knocked him to the ground and spread his small body out on top of him, to protect him. The house father understood: the German shepherds that accompanied Nazi guards had been used to attack, herd, and mutilate people in the concentration camp where this young boy had lost everything. . . .

"Jamaica," I said, "when people get to be friends, they look out for each other. Lots of days I try to look out for you; today you're looking out for me. Thank you."

Jamaica nodded. "Thas okay, Auntie." She began to sing along with Madonna.

We went directly to the mask store and bought the most frightening mask Jamaica could find. It had fangs for teeth, wrinkled and bloody-looking skin, and one completely white eye—no pupil, no iris. Then we went to my house and looked through the trunk full of old costumes. Halloween had been an important holiday to my children when they were young. They loved the fun and fantasy of marching in the annual Greenwich Village Halloween Parade and every year we had worked together to create elaborate costumes. Jamaica was delighted to sift through them and ask me what Samantha and Benjamin had been for Halloween when they were her age. She tried on all the costumes and paraded in front of the mirror as a silver moon, John Travolta, a monster, a witch, a Playboy bunny, Frankenstein, and the Bride of Frankenstein. Finally she chose a long black cape-dress that Samantha had worn to be a sorcerer. To complete the costume we went to a cheap wig shop on Fourteenth Street. Jamaica tried on every wig. She pranced around, looked in the mirror, flipped her head, and asked me how I liked each one.

"Auntie, do I look like a hooker?" Jamaica stood up straight, stuck out her chest, and turned slowly, the long blond hair resting on her tiny shoulders. "I can be that if I want," she said to me, and to the astonished Asian shopkeeper. I glanced over at the woman, smiled at her, and hoped she didn't understand.

"You said you want to be scary. That's not scary enough."

Jamaica agreed. She chose a waist-length wig of straight jet-black hair, which she said she could comb partly over her face.

When we returned to my house, I looked through my closet and gave Jamaica an old pair of black high heels, which she stuffed with newspaper and wore back to Hilltop in the car. We arranged everything for her costume, packed up all her things, and were just about to leave when I noticed a bulge underneath her blouse.

"Jamaica, what have you got in there?"

"Nuthin." She turned her back to me as she put on her jacket.

"You've got something—show me what it is."

While I was out of the room, Jamaica had stuffed all the food she could gather into the space between her jeans, sweatshirt, and body, and tightened her jacket around it. She had cereal, cookies, raisin boxes, and a piece of cold chicken. She threw it all down on the floor, put her hand on her hip, and glared at me.

"Jamaica," I said, "you can't just take things, I've told you before. You have to ask me. Let's see what you have there."

Jamaica continued to glare as I told her to take all the food she had hidden in her clothing and put it on the table. We would look at it, see what she could have, and pack it up in a bag to take back to Hilltop. I told her that she could have almost any food in the house if she asked me, but I didn't want her to take anything from the house unless we decided she could. Once again I said that taking anything without permission was stealing, and I didn't like people stealing from me—it made me mad at them. I told her I didn't want to be mad at her, so she had better stop stealing from me.

"I can have the whole box of Cheerios," Jamaica asked, "an the piece of chicken?"

"You can have the whole box, and either this chicken or the Kentucky Fried meal I said we would buy to eat on the way back."

"Yes!" Jamaica dove under the sink, where the paper bags are kept. "Kentucky Fried, these Cheerios, an this bag of cookies."

"I want some cookies, too—you have to leave some for me. Half for you, half for me—you divide."

Jamaica spread the cookies out on the table, and carefully and fairly she put one in her bowl, one in mine, until they were evenly divided. Then she put her half in the cookie bag, packed it up with her other things, and said, "I promise Tanika I be bringin back food for us to eat, so don't tell Staff I got stuff when we get back or they be eatin it all. Thas what they do—they steals you food." She rolled her eyes and shook her head in disgust at the thieves.

IT WAS DARK and cold as we walked from the parking lot to the cottage. No one was outside. Jamaica held my hand. "You be scared?" she asked as we passed a deserted building. "Boys say they be ghostis in there—maybe you should carry me in you arms like a baby. Ghostis don't be botherin wit no babies." We continued to walk along holding hands.

Inside the cottage, Jamaica went directly down the hall to her room. I went to the kitchen to tell Staff we were back. Staff nodded and went on supervising the girls cleaning up after supper. I headed down the hall, to find Jamaica's door shut. When I knocked, she asked who it was, then let me in and went on whispering to Tanika. Tanika was completely dressed in Jamaica's Halloween costume. Plans were being made to scare the other girls while they were watching TV. I said good-bye to Jamaica and told her I thought she had made a great witch costume for Halloween.

THE DAY AFTER HALLOWEEN, at about ten in the morning, the phone rang in my office. It was Miss Higby, laughing. She told me that Jamaica had just burst in to tell her she had to call me, because something was very important and she could not wait. She handed the phone to Jamaica.

In a breathless, low voice, almost a whisper, Jamaica said, "Auntie, guess what—I won the scaryis in the whole school. At the party, I be goin around jumpin out at people an gettin right in they face when they wasn't lookin. Miss Higby almos fell out when I jump at her from up on the stage—right, Miss Higby? Then they be givin out prizes, an they call my name out for the scaryis in the whole school. 'Jamaica Thomas' they say, 'you git you ass up here, cause you be the scaryis they is.' No way wuz I gonna go up on that big ol stage by myself. They keep callin and callin an I be tryin to hide behin the curtains when Tanika an everyone done drag me out on the stage. The big ol teacher, he hol me up high in he arms an say this be the scaryis costume in the whole big school. Everyone be clappin and hollerin an stuff, makin those funny kind of whistles. I be tryin to run away. Then they give me a prize—a big dog for my bed, white and has black spots like that movie dog. I call it Ghostis after my costume. Auntie, I can keep all the things from my costume—my shoes, my hair, my maskis, an even the dress of Samantha?"

"Sure, you can keep everything—looks like you put together a scary costume. That's great, Jamaica, the scariest in the whole school. All that Chucky practice must have helped you out. I'm glad you won—and I'm glad you called to tell me."

"Me too, Auntie. Miss Higby say I gotta to go, I be talkin too much."

Miss Higby took the phone. "That child sure is happy today. She's ten feet tall."

I wiped my eyes, hung up the phone, and went back to work.

Chapter 16

A few days later, Miss Higby phoned again.

"Even though it's nearly a month off, the kids up here are talk-ing about Thanksgiving already. Jamaica said she's going home with you for the holiday—is that true?" It was not. I wouldn't be in New York for Thanksgiving. I was going to Boston, to spend the holiday with my family. Miss Higby replied that was fine; she had wanted to know if I did want Jamaica, so that she could have made plans and applied for permission. She went on to say that anyway I would not have been permitted to take Jamaica out of state.

Her call made me face the guilt I had been pushing away. I knew the holidays were coming, and I knew I didn't want to be with Jamaica on either Thanksgiving or Christmas. Last year I had not known her well enough for this to be an issue. This year I knew her quite well; we had spent many days together. I knew I was the only person she could even imagine spending the hol-idays with. I knew she would want to come to my home, and I knew I didn't want to be with her. I wanted to spend my holidays with my family alone, and enjoy them, without her.

In the past few weeks, Jamaica had once again spent afternoons and weekends at my home. Being with her was exhaust-ing. She was a full-time job, requiring my undivided attention, leaving no room for anything or anyone else. She had to be watched constantly for fear she might harm herself or other peo-ple. She played with matches, leaned out of windows, left the stove on, stole anything not nailed down, dashed into streets, and threw furious temper tantrums, involving kicking, spitting, and biting, when she didn't get her way. She never flushed the toilet. Once, after I went to bed, I checked to see that Jamaica was asleep only to find she was up, had fixed herself some food, and was watching porno on cable.

When my daughter, Samantha, was home from college she enjoyed playing with Jamaica. But after she and Samantha had finished playing and Samantha wanted to be with her friends, Ja-maica wouldn't leave them alone. She followed them, held on to their arms, and continually knocked on Samantha's door until she was let in. Not only did I have to protect her, but I had to protect others from her. She could not keep her distance from the teenage boys who in coming to the house to visit my son be-came the unwilling and embarrassed targets of her amorous ad-vances. She leaped up on them and entwined herself around them, holding on with a death grip, laughing wildly. When a boy tried to take one of her arms from around his neck, she simply put it back. Trying to peel her off turned into a game she was de-termined to win. The only way to win was to hold on to her and keep her from starting.

What always worked best was spending time together alone, with me completely available and with no distractions or needs, my own or other family members', to attend to. Then we had fun: we sang, read stories, went to movies, picked out and bought presents for her cottage, played in the park, drank coffee at the Bagel Shop, and rode bicycles around the neighborhood. I was the appreciative audience for her singing. She was eager to show off new knowledge—letters she could write and words she could spell. She was particularly proud to ask, once she learned it, whether I knew the difference between deciduous and evergreen trees.

Still, being with her required nonstop vigilance and at times was grueling work. It was not possible to go about life with any semblance of calm and order. Jamaica created havoc; she could not find order in herself or take it from her surroundings. She showed little real affection and only temporary attachment. She was always in search of the hand that might offer more. After a birthday party for a friend's child during which Jamaica had spent considerable time engaged with the aunt of the birthday girl, she refused to leave, had a temper tantrum, broke dishes, and held on to the hand of the newfound stranger/friend. She wanted to go home with this woman and stay with her for the rest of the weekend. After I had pried her off the woman, helped clean up the mess she had made, and dragged her, party hat and all, out of the door, I would have been glad to send her back to Hilltop and never see her again.

Jamaica's frequent betrayals stung me. She did not seem to feel the reciprocal emotions that connect people. Just when I was feeling close to her, she would disregard me or discard me without a second thought. She would seem to feel some connection to me, some affection, and then something would happen to indicate that she felt little or nothing for me or anyone else. The only thing she seemed to grasp was the danger of losing something she wanted to have.

After the incident at the party I felt truly enraged. It had been particularly difficult to get her that weekend: freezing rains and flooding had made the roads impassable on Friday. Because I had told her about the party and promised we could attend, I had driven up on Saturday. The roads were still dangerous, and once I arrived, I found that despite my call to the office to tell them when I would be arriving, Staff had either not been notified or had decided I was not coming. In any case, Jamaica was not there—she had left campus to go ice skating, and she would not

be back for three hours. I either had to wait upstate or go home
without her. When I told Staff that I was expecting to take Jamaica home, she said without so much as a glance in my direction, that I could wait in the cafeteria if I felt like it.

As I had already planned to be with Jamaica this weekend and
I did not want to disappoint her, I decided to wait in town and
return when the three hours were up and, I hoped, she would be
back at the school. I drove into town, looked around, bought a
newspaper, and sat down to read. An hour passed. There was little to do—no bookstore, no park to walk in. The day was cold,
foggy, and damp as I walked up and down the one main street,
looking in store windows. Spotting a beauty shop, I decided that
something good would come of this: for the first time in years, I
would have a facial and manicure. This would take up at least an
hour. I joined in the banter of women sitting under dryers, heard
local news, tragedy, and gossip, and picked out the most muted
color available for my long-neglected nails. I bought some
doughnuts to eat on the ride home—coconut for Jamaica, cinnamon for me—and went back to the school to await her return.

After about an hour, four hours after I had first arrived, the big
yellow school bus rolled in. Children raced off the bus, pushing,
laughing, talking loudly. Jamaica and Tanika came off together.
They ran over to me when they saw the car, and both got in.

"Less go," Jamaica said. "We goin to you house—right?"

"Jamaica," I said, "did you remember I was coming to get you
today? Did Miss Higby tell you I was coming today because the
storm was too bad yesterday?"

Jamaica nodded. "Miss Higby tell me you be comin today. I
know you be here."

"Why didn't you wait for me, if you knew I was coming?"

"Staff tell me you comin and to stay back in the cottage, but I
didn't want to miss skatin, so I jus jump on the bus wit Tanika,
and no one say nuthin to me. I didn't want to miss all the fun."

"But what if I hadn't waited for you? What if I had just gone
home when I found out you weren't waiting for me?"

Jamaica shrugged her shoulders, and said nothing.

I was about to blow up. I had waited four hours for her, and I could see that Jamaica had absolutely no concern about what she had done. Perhaps, if I had not come at all, she would have gone off skating and not even missed me.

Later, as we walked home from the party, I thought about all that had happened on this day. I'd requested permission to bring her back in the morning so that she could stay out later and have fun at the party, but now I wished I were driving her back to the school that night. I felt like screaming at her, telling her that if she wanted to go home with the woman from the party, she should have, and that from now on that woman could visit her, take her home on weekends, take her out for the day. Instead, I gained control and told Jamaica that when she came to see me for a weekend, she had to wait for me at the cottage: next time I wouldn't wait for her. And if she came to see me, she was going to stay with me, not try to go home with someone else. If she didn't want to do these things, I told her, she did not have to come at all.

Jamaica tapped her foot and shot me her defiant, narrow-eyed glare, which seemed filled with rage and loathing. She saw me as standing in the way of her getting what she wanted when something better came along.

Over the past year, since Jamaica had been been spending time at my home, both knowledgeable professional friends and parents who had raised children had expressed their fear and dislike of her. They began to offer me unsolicited protective advice, and pointed out what they viewed as irreversible sociopathic traits. One old school friend, a child psychiatrist, admonished me to get out as soon as possible. "This kid is really bad news—deprived, angry, without an ounce of empathy or guilt, completely lost. She seems psychopathic—the kind of person who might grow up to slit people's throats and not even blink." She ended with a scary prophecy: "If you stay involved with her, she will hurt you more than you could ever possibly hurt her." Children did not

want to play with her. She was bossy, grabbed toys, and interrupted the games she was losing by quitting or by throwing game
pieces on the floor.

I knew that everything my friends said held some truth. I
couldn't expect people to like Jamaica when I often didn't like
her myself. Around most people she was terrible. Almost no one
saw the other side of her, the side that would only come out when
she was relaxed and we were alone. We had spent a lot of time
alone together, and despite our many bad days, her displays of
kindness, desire to belong to someone, and gutsy survival against
all odds mattered to me. I remained fond of her and felt protective. I worried about her physical and emotional well-being.

"Auntie," she asked on our way back to Hilltop the morning
after the party, "do you like me?"

"I do—I like you a lot."

"Thas good, cause Staff say I be hateful. They be sayin I'm a
real bad kid."

"They're wrong, Jamaica—it's not true. You're a good kid.
Sometimes you do get a little frisky and people get mad at you. I
get mad at you sometimes."

"I be frisky that day I bite you arm."

"You were very frisky that day, and I was very mad at you. I was
very mad at you yesterday, too, when you didn't wait for me at
the school and then when you broke things and threw things
around at the party."

"I be glad I didn't bite you more or make you madder at me,
cause then maybe you be so mad you never want to see me no
more an I wouldn't be ridin wit you now in my ol car listenin to
music."

"I was mad at you. But I like you, so I wanted to get over it.
I'm not mad at you at all anymore."

Jamaica nodded. "I know. I be glad we frens an I didn't hurt
you heart like I did Miss Pope."

Still, by this time I had realized I absolutely could never live
with Jamaica. To live with her would change my life too drasti-

cally, in a way I did not want it to change. My sense of self-preservation and my protectiveness of my family were very strong. I had never set out to bring another child into our family. I didn't want one, and I didn't want Jamaica to take over my life or interfere any more with my family's lives than she already had. I wanted to be a bridge to another life for her, but not to sacrifice too much of my own. Jerry was kind to her, but he had no desire for another child, and if he had, it would not have been for a child as difficult as Jamaica.

As time went on and it didn't appear that any permanent plan was being made for her future, Jerry became concerned about what would happen if only I remained involved with Jamaica year after year as she grew older and things got worse. He felt it might be better to see her less now, to taper off, so that she did not count on me more and more and expect from me what I did not want to give. He believed that Jamaica would simply forget about me and go on in her life, taking whatever was available to her from whoever was there to give it.

The approaching holidays brought Jamaica's situation to a crisis point in my mind. I knew that unless I did something her situation would remain as unstable as it now was, and that what Jerry said would be true: she would count on me more and more for things I could not give and did not want to give. I listened to what friends and family thought I should do, while intent on trying to create my own plan. Despite what everyone told me, I could not walk away and leave Jamaica hanging on her cliff of unpredictable, changing placements. Even if she forgot about me completely, I would worry about her. I would worry about the little girl who emerged from under her cold and ruthless character, giggled, and was happy for a moment or two. She was still nine—I wanted her to have a chance.

I went over and over all the options. I didn't think an ordinary foster home placement would work—Jamaica was just too hard to be around for any length of time. There was little or no chance she would be adopted: she was defiant, not appealing.

The permanence she needed would not come through ordinary channels. Though I kept up with my Big Sister companion role, I now had another focus. I didn't want to leave the planning for Jamaica's future up to Hilltop. I would try to devise and put into action a life plan for her that might give her a chance to put down roots and make up for her so far stunted growth.

A self-righteous psychoanalytic colleague asked a question that implied I had some hidden pathology. It oozed disdain and angered me. "What do you want to do something like that for?"

"Maybe Freud was right when he said that character is destiny," I retorted. I didn't worry I was becoming a martyr—I was not headed for the life of Mother Teresa. I believed I could find a way out of my dilemma without Jamaica or me being hurt. When times with Jamaica were especially difficult, I did wonder what lay under the obvious, what might have been my underlying unconsious motivation. But I didn't really care much about that, and I never wanted to use those speculations in order to get myself out of sticking with her.

My mother watched this struggle from afar. She had met Jamaica once, when they were both visiting me, and she saw how difficult Jamaica could be. When I told her how seemingly impossible it was to help her get settled into a permanent, decent living arrangment, she told me she thought I would figure it out. Then she added—with what I knew to be her sanction and her belief in how things should be—"You won't walk away from the child; it's not in your nature." To illustrate what she felt was "my nature," she reminded me of something I had long forgotten.

Early in the fall of my sixth-grade year, Mrs. Morris, my teacher at the Jonas Perkins Elementary School, asked me to stay behind as the others left for recess in the yard. She told me that Becky Ward needed a friend. Becky was extremely unattractive. She was at least two heads taller than the rest of us, walked in a strange shuffle, and had stringy hair that hung over her eyes. She was retarded, and she was so shy she sank into herself. She was always on the edge of things, until after the sixth grade she disappeared into the room in the basement of our junior high school and entered "special class."

Mrs. Morris sat me down at the side of her desk, folded her hands, and looked at me. She said she was telling me about Becky because she felt I could keep our talk a secret and that I could and would convince the other girls in our class to be nice to her, include her, eat lunch with her, invite her to parties. She asked if I knew what a leper was. I did. I had a green pig bank from my church. I put all my pennies in it to give to the United Methodist mission fund for aid to lepers. It was getting heavy, I told her. She nodded approval, and although I didn't get the connection between Becky Ward and lepers, I knew she was asking me to do something that should be done.

"Becky is not as smart, as pretty, or as able as the rest of you," she told me. I nodded. It was a woman-to-woman conversation. I felt pride in the seriousness and the confidence Mrs. Morris showed in me, and I became determined to make the shunners and hecklers come around. I began right away, by inviting Becky to be my fire drill partner. Although I felt a lot more shaky as I wobbled down the three flights of open fire escape stairs attached to the back of the old wooden school building, and I missed my friend Nancy's firm hand in mine, I knew I would not turn back—trust had been placed in me. I would keep on track.

But Mrs. Morris was slightly wrong about me: I broke the confidence. I told one person, my mother. "That's my girl," my mother said. And I knew nothing could have made her prouder.

Knowing that I was not going to take Jamaica for the holidays, I asked Miss Higby what happened to most of the kids during the holiday season. She said it depended on whether the children had any relatives who wanted them. If they were waiting for foster home placement or adoption, they could sometimes go to those homes for trial visits.

"Don't you worry," she said in an cheerful voice. "Jamaica will not be alone here—there are lots of kids like her and Tanika. We plan a program for the holidays, have a big Thanksgiving dinner, maybe move all the kids who are left into one or two cottages so more Staff can have off. It is like a holiday for the kids here, too."

I hung up and that night had the following dream:

A young brown colt was tied to my car. I took it to the barn where I kept my other horses. The horses frolicked in the pasture, chasing each other, leaping straight into the air.

I saw my friends in the distance; they called to me, and I went off with them. I left the colt tied to my car but forgot to tell my aunt about it. When I came back the colt was dead, lying flat on the ground, shriveled up into a piece of brittle leather. I started to sob and to call, "Auntie, Auntie." No one came. When I awoke I was still sobbing.

The next morning I called Miss Higby and told her I would like to make an appointment to talk with her. I had some ideas and questions about permanent planning for Jamaica. I had made some inquiries of people in the Bureau of Child Welfare and had come up with questions about guardianship that I wanted to discuss. We agreed to meet on Friday, before I took Jamaica for the weekend.

Chapter 17

Miss Higby listened carefully as I told her my thoughts. I had come to believe that Jamaica would thrive best in a good residential school that offered strong psychological and educational programs. I said that although a residential treatment center such as Hilltop offered such services, I could see that her stay here would be short—after a certain mandated period, she would leave for another placement. This, it appeared, could and likely would happen over and over, thus putting Jamaica through an endless chain of fragmented experiences, new placements, new social adjustments, new educational programs, until she was old enough to be out of the system, at which point she would likely be in worse shape emotionally than she already was and still not be qualified to do anything. I told Miss Higby that the way things were going for Jamaica, she would never be able to get attached to anything or anyone.

But, I thought, if I could apply for and obtain legal guardianship, I could find a residential school and use the money now spent on her at Hilltop or that would be spent on foster care to pay for her education. As her guardian, I would have a say in plans made for her, with the goal of obtaining consistency in her life. I thought that if I could be involved with her in this way, I would be able to be more effective in seeing to it that she got what she needed.

Miss Higby listened, smiled, and shook her head. "It won't work. Policy is to find homes for these children—hopefully, adoptive homes, but if that is not possible, foster homes or as a last resort a good group home. Jamaica needs a family."

"Jamaica has needed a family for ten years," I replied. "It appears to me that she is getting further and further away from ever being able to be in a family and that as she waits she becomes more disturbed, more hollow, and less attached to anything or anyone. She is moved and buffeted about in such a way that she never has anything to count on."

"It looks like she can count on you—that's more than a lot of kids here have."

"She can't count on me enough, because I have no real power to do anything for her. I'm not a relative and I don't want to adopt her or to take her as a foster child. If I thought she had a chance at being adopted or at having a successful foster care experience, I would never suggest this. I'm no longer sure either of those would even give her the attention, structure, and consistency she needs, but that's irrelevant—we both know Jamaica is unlikely to have either one. She is considered undesirable for adoption and is a poor risk for foster care. She had it once and she failed miserably, just as she failed in the Brooklyn group home. A special-needs boarding school for six to eight years with home visits to me, vacations, and summer plans made according to what is best for her would seem to me to offer consistency. I don't believe she is going to get anything better anywhere else."

"You know, Miss Atkins, I'll be straight with you. We want her with an Afro-American family. We try to place all our children in families of the same race. It is the policy, and also adjustment is so much easier on the child when she's not the different one in a family."

"I agree with you, but there don't seem to be any people, white or black, in the wings here waiting to assume responsibility for Jamaica."

Miss Higby began to look at her watch. "Jamaica is on the list of children available for both adoption and foster placement. She will begin to be interviewed by placement agencies before too long. We will try to get her placed—that's the treatment plan for her. I would not recommend your plan; as a placement plan it would take her out of the system which still might find her a home."

"Taking her out of a system that we both know is unlikely to find her a permanent home is exactly what I think she needs. Lots of money is being spent on her care, but as far as I can see it is being wasted. She could settle in at a school and not have to keep getting bounced around. I'd like to try to see to that. Even if you could find a foster care or adoption placement for her, she'd act up, the placement would fail, and she'd likely be sent somewhere to await another attempt at placement. These attempts and failures could happen over and over again until she's eighteen or has run away and disappeared. With Jamaica's track record, no one will even want to bother to look. I think what I am offering to do would give her a better chance. Either that or keep her here through high school."

"That's not going to happen," Miss Higby replied. "We hope to find a placement for her by spring."

Miss Higby seemed convinced that Jamaica could be placed, and as she was new to this work, she had not had the experiences that might have made her more pessimistic.

I put on my coat and went over to the cottage to wait for Jamaica to return from school. She arrived hand in hand with Tanika. Both girls were laughing and whispering. "Tanika comin too," Jamaica announced. "I toll her she could."

Tanika was looking so hopeful, it was hard to tell her she couldn't come. When I explained we had no permission to take her, she shrugged her shoulders slightly and looked sad.

Jamaica whispered to her some more; then Tanika left and Jamaica and I went to her room to pack up some clothing for the
weekend. We couldn't find any clean clothing in her drawers.
After her Chucky shirt got lost in the wash, Jamaica had no faith
that the laundry would return anything, so each day she stuffed
whatever she had been wearing right back into the drawers. I
told her to bring socks, underwear, a blouse, jeans, and pajamas;
we would do a load of wash when we got to my house. Jamaica
threw her belongings into a pillowcase. Where was the duffel
bag I had given her the previous week to carry back her Halloween costume? She shrugged and said, "Stole, I guess."

Jamaica put her bony little hand over my eyes as I opened the
car door. "Jus drive, Auntie," she said. She jumped in ahead of
me, scooted over the gear shift, and began to settle into her routine of setting up her tapes, closing her eyes, and telling me to let
her know when we had passed the stone pillars at the entrance.
Jamaica turned up the music, but not high enough to mask the
muffled giggles from the backseat. We had just started to turn
out of the driveway at the end of the row of cottages when I
turned around to see a sneaker under the pillowcase Jamaica had
stuffed with clothing and thrown in the back.

"I think we have a little company with us, Jamaica. I'd better
stop the car and take a look."

"You be crazy—ain't nobody here but you an me. Jus drive, it
be gettin late."

"I'd better take a look. We wouldn't want anybody to jump out
and surprise us when we're driving along. I might get scared and
crash the car."

"You be a fool, Tanika. I toll you not to make a sound. Here
you done gone an spoil our whole plan. Now you have to stay
here an can't be goin into Auntie house. You be one stupid nig-
ger. Get out the car an outta my face."

"Jamaica, don't talk to Tanika like that. You know she can't
come to my house. I told you I have no permission to take her. If
she left, hidden in the car like this, all of us would get into trou-

ble and neither of you would be able to leave the school. Tanika, sit up and I'll drive you back to the cottage."

"You be really stupid, Tanika. No one was gonna know, Auntie. I plan to hide her in my room in you house an I feed her some of the food I sneak up to her. We come back to school an jus slide her right back in. Some of the big kids tell how they go AWOL —thas what me an Tanika be plannin. They don't do nuthin to you for AWOL, jus make you stay on grounds an I be stayin anyway, so I don't care."

We let Tanika off back at the cottage, and since I didn't think she had been gone long enough to be in trouble for leaving without permission, I let her go inside alone before we started again for New York City.

Jamaica again closed her eyes and asked me to tell her when we passed the stone pillars. She was silent as we drove down the hills onto the entrance to the parkway. "I be missin Tanika. I really want her to come wit me. Don't you go tellin Staff or anythin, but me an Tanika in love. Sometimes at night she come into my bed or I go into her bed an we be kissin an pattin each other booty, rubbin all over." Jamaica closed her eyes. "It feel so good—I love kissin Tanika, except sometimes when she have this bad breathis. It really stink an I don't want her tongue all over me. Her breathis smell just like my momma say some men's breathis smell, like camel breathis, an I don't want to be kissin any of that ol camel breathis—it be really nasty. Tanika an me gonna live together when we big, we be plannin how we git us a house an stuff.

"Auntie, I be tellin you me an Tanika's secret—you ain't gonna be telling Staff on me. They be takin Tanika or me an puttin us away in some other cottage an we never see each other again. Thas what happen to two girls Staff say were lesbos. I ain't no lesbos, me an Tanika jus in love.

"You not be telling Staff, right, Auntie? This be a secret of you, me, an Tanika."

"Don't worry, I won't tell Staff. I don't want you to get into any more trouble than you already are in."

Jamaica nodded. "I jus like the way I feel with Tanika, all warm an cozy like she my mother when I used to lay on up in her legs. Tanika an me say we be family an stuff. You like Tanika?"

I said I did like Tanika. I told Jamaica I thought Tanika had a nice smile and a real funny laugh, so that when she laughed I wanted to laugh too.

Jamaica looked very serious; she thought for a moment and then replied, "She do, she really do."

We rode along, the silence occasionally being broken by Jamaica's singing along with Bob Marley: "I shot the sheriff, but I didn't shoot the dep u dee."

Jamaica and I had some of our best moments as we rode along in the car, me driving and Jamaica singing softly to herself, making expressive head movements, whispering tender phrases, closing her eyes, sometimes telling me her secrets. I was listening to her sing and also thinking about my conversation with Miss Higby, when suddenly I had a new idea.

"Jamaica, if I can find Miss Pope and if she will agree to see us, would you like to visit her?"

Jamaica turned her head very slowly, inching her face toward me. For a moment she just glared, then she said, "If she don't be hatin me, I be there in one hot minute."

I said, "I'll try."

Jamaica replied, "You better!"

Chapter 18

I felt an increasing sense of urgency. Thanksgiving was two and a half weeks away, and even though Miss Higby had tried to reassure me that Jamaica would be all right over the holiday, I did not want her to have to remain at Hilltop when the school emptied out. Also, I knew that plans were once again afoot to find another placement for her, and I feared she had little time left before she was shuttled into something new. I thought I should act swiftly. First thing Monday morning, I called an old friend at Mercy, unfolded my plan, and asked a favor: would she search the records for the name, address, and phone number of Miss Pope? I wanted to see if there was any hope of a reconciliation. Miss Pope had had an interest in taking a foster child in the past; I wondered if she might again. I also knew that the dodgy history Miss Pope and Jamaica had experienced together might have left Miss Pope never wanting to see her again. When I weighed that possibility against the reality that there were absolutely no other options, it seemed worth taking this single chance to reconnect Jamaica with the only person I knew of who had meaning to her before, once again, she was cast to the winds.

By noon I was on the phone with Miss Pope.

"Miss Pope, my name is Linda Atkins, and I'm calling because I am a friend of Jamaica Thomas." I explained how I had met Jamaica at Mercy and how I'd stayed involved with her as she went from one placement to another.

There was silence on the other end of the line, then a cautious and questioning "Yes?"

"I'm calling you because ever since I met Jamaica, I've known about you. The first time I took her out for a walk, we stopped for a soda. She didn't want a soda; she wanted coffee just the way she used to sit and drink it with you—in her own cup, lots of sugar, and not too much milk. I knew right away that she had a strong connection to you, that she missed your home. She liked to talk about you—the way you make steak with A.1 sauce and set out the plates on the table in front of the TV, how she would sit on your lap and eat supper while you watched your programs together. The time she spent with you, your children, and your grandchildren is the only recollection of happy home life she has. She is forever telling me, 'I bet you can't do it like Miss Pope.' The truth is, I can't."

"I'll be frank with you," Miss Pope replied. "That skinny little girl brought me nothing but trouble. I am not looking to see her again. I took in a foster child because I needed the money for my mortgage and I thought it would be nice to have some company—a child about to talk to and take care of, now that my own family is grown. I went to the agency, I got Jamaica, and my troubles began. At first I thought, 'This child is just too wild, too hepped up and angry at the drop of a hat for an old lady to be chasing after.' Yet, when the social worker told me what her life had been, I felt sorry for her and decided I would do God's work, give it a try. Once I met her and knew she had no one looking out for her, no mother to love and take care of her bad self, I couldn't see myself sending her away when there was no place and no person on earth who wanted her. I thought with time we could work things out. 'What harm can she do?' I thought. 'She is only a child.'

"Right from the beginning she was bad. She stole things, never minded anything I told her to do, cursed at everyone, threw herself all over men in a way that was more like a woman than a little girl. She had never spent a day in school and was so far behind she had to be put into a special class. Even that was difficult—the teacher called me in all the time to tell me she could not sit still for more than five seconds.

"She was a pathetic little thing when she came to me. Her hair was all natty and her body full of scabs and scars. At night she would scream so loud I thought she was being killed. I'd rush in and find her shivering, shaking, and sobbing in her sleep. I would pick her up, take her in bed with me, and comfort her. I thought after a few months she was coming along. She liked staying with me, sitting on my lap, and watching TV, and she seemed to be settling into the family. I found a few things she could do to help out and be part of family life, like setting up the table and feeding the cat, who she loved. She liked to work alongside me, to help me. She wasn't good at picking up after herself, but I figured she was still young, that when she got a bit older she would learn.

"Then, I suppose you know the rest. She accused Johnny, my boyfriend, of putting his hands on her. Of course it wasn't true, but by the time we proved it, we had all been through the mill. I began to wish I had never laid eyes on that child. Johnny like to had a heart attack. He is a good man, a family man—nothing like this had ever happened to him. So I was scared for all of us that we would be drug into court or such. Jamaica did speak out, she said nothing had really happened, that she was just playing. But I was worried, and I went to try to get help for her at the agency who sent her to me. No sooner had I gone there and told them what had happened than the agency launched a big investigation of the charges Jamaica had already denied. They took her away from my home and treated me and my boyfriend like we was criminals. It felt dirty. They would not even let me visit her, and I had been the one to call them. It wasn't worth the upset to me, so I just backed away from the whole thing and let nature take its course. You know, despite the fact that we were all cleared and that I brought her in for help, they never called to ask me to take her back. That left a bad taste, like them saying I was not good for her, like there was still suspicion.

"From time to time something reminds me of that skinny little thing. I wonder how she is and I wish it could have turned out better. She was tough, though. She would just stare me down. At times I liked her and we had some good times. At other times I had no more patience. I missed her at first, but then life seemed so much better, so calm and ordinary with her gone, that I knew I was better off without her."

"Miss Pope, I'm glad to be talking to you, to finally talk to someone who really knows Jamaica. I've spent lots of time with her, and you are the only one I know who feels just like I do. I like her a lot sometimes, but at other times I've had it with her and I feel I never want to see her again. She can be so mean and ungrateful. The way I know she misses you comes out in the ways that she is nasty to me. One night I made her some fried chicken. She stuck her fork into the chicken, poked around at the crust, then asked, 'You be callin this fried chicken?' Without another word she took her plate, walked to the garbage can, dumped the chicken in the garbage, and stood there with her hand on her hip, shaking her head in disbelief. 'Miss Pope be knowin how to make fried chicken—I can't be eatin this shit.' "

Miss Pope chuckled. "That's Jamaica to a T. The child did love my food—she ate and ate. I never saw another child who could eat as much as Jamaica, and her being so skinny and all. It was like she was eating for all the meals she missed. But what good did it do? It was like spitting in the wind—nothing sticks, but it comes right back in your face. It came back in my face with a slap."

I agreed. "It's hard with her; it often seems that nothing you do really matters. After a while you begin to think, 'Why should I care?' But you don't want to be the next person to leave her either."

"My boyfriend told me to keep away from her, that she will end up hurting everyone in my family. I don't know if I believe that, but I do believe she'll never do us any good, that it might just be too hopeless with her. I have two new foster children now, twins from the agency. They are crack babies; both have been abused. Sometimes their mother left them alone for days at a time. Yet these little boys are nothing like Jamaica—they are sweet children. Darius and Julio are completely the opposite of Jamaica. They appreciate things. They are sweet to me—it's Grandma this, Grandma that. I feel love coming from their little hearts. I feel they want to kiss and hug me, where all Jamaica wanted to do was bite me and look for what my hand held out to give her next."

"Jamaica is different from other children, even other children who have had hard lives. With Jamaica it is not so much what you do but what you have to try to *undo* that makes life with her so impossible, so frustrating and enraging."

"That's a good way of saying it," Miss Pope replied. "How is she, anyway—what is going to happen to her?"

"She's up at Hilltop now. It's an upstate residential school for kids with lots of problems. She's okay there—a little rough around the edges, I'd say, getting into trouble, learning too much she shouldn't be learning from the older kids and trying not to get caught doing things she shouldn't be doing. She is still lost. There is no real plan for her. The way it looks, she'll stay there until time runs out or the school can find a place for her—they tell me adoption or a foster home."

"Doesn't seem likely to me. She's too much trouble, and people discover that fact real fast."

"I told that to the social worker. It doesn't seem likely to me, either. I see her about every other weekend, and I take her to my house overnight. How would you like a visitor some Saturday afternoon?"

Miss Pope was quiet. "I don't hate her, but I don't know—

she is not a welcome addition. It's likely best to leave well enough be."

"When I talked to her and told her I was going to see if I could find you, she said she would like to see you if you didn't hate her. She is well aware that she caused you lots of trouble and that you might never want to see her again. She told me she hurt your heart."

For a few moments Miss Pope was silent. Then she went on: "It's a strange thing—it is like I am afraid of her. Even though she is a small child, she has so little regard for me that I feel shaky in having her around. Yet another part of me says to be generous, let the child come by, hide all my money, keep the men away, and treat her like the young child she is. I really would like to see her, to say hello to her. You can bring her by the copy store some Saturday, if you want—no harm can come from that. It might even be good to let her know that people can have forgiveness in their hearts for her. Maybe it will help her be less hardhearted."

"I had better not tell her this when we are driving in the car. Jamaica will go wild—I can see her screaming and jumping and grabbing the wheel to make me drive to see you immediately. She told me if you would let her come she would be there in 'one hot minute.' "

Again Miss Pope chuckled. "Maybe I'm an old fool who's not too smart about what's good for her, but I feel relief in knowing where she is. I stopped myself from thinking about her and worrying about her the way you do about a child. I am very glad you called. Something in me stayed bothered by her disappearance, like a child I had care of was just taken away from my protection and help. I've prayed for her often. Despite everything that happened, I still can't shake my feeling of responsibility for her."

"Neither can I," I replied. "Neither can I."

Chapter 19

Later that week I called Miss Pope to ask her if I could bring Jamaica to the copy store on Saturday afternoon. She told me to bring her in the early afternoon, after lunch, when the store was usually not too busy. I had my eye on the calendar: there were two more weekends before Thanksgiving. I wanted to see if it was possible for Jamaica to visit Miss Pope for the holiday.

It was the Friday of a weekend visit. Miss Higby had called during the week to say that if Jamaica was going to continue to come to my house on weekends, a social worker had to make a home visit to see where she was going to sleep and whether the house was appropriate to accommodate a child. She said that the social worker doing the investigation could bring Jamaica into the city with the other children going on weekend visits, drop her off at my house, and save me a trip. I readily agreed, but I wondered why this visit was being made now. It seemed a day late and a dollar short, given the fact that Jamaica had been visiting for over a year. Miss Higby told me it was just routine, that Hilltop had to record that they had made a visit and approved my home. I wondered whether there was any other reason; given what I had been told of Jamaica's history with Miss Pope, I was concerned and eager to know if there was a hidden agenda behind this visit.

It was dusk when the sound of our loud doorbell ringing nonstop heralded Jamaica's arrival. She burst in past me without greeting, took off her coat, and with great authority told the two young women who had emerged from the school van and were just climbing the front stoop to follow her. I introduced myself to them. Another woman sat in the driver's seat of the van; three other children played in back.

The social workers were both Hispanic about twenty-five to thirty, dressed in jogging suits and sneakers. One wore a long overcoat, the other a ski jacket. When I asked to take their coats, they declined, saying they would only stay for a moment; other children had to be delivered to homes in Queens and Brooklyn.

"Come on wit me," Jamaica directed. "I be showin you everything. Here come the dog—he be called Guinness an he play ball real good."

Guinness came racing in to greet her, his tail wagging. She leaned down, put her arms around his big yellow neck, and began to kiss him on his head.

"Jamaica, get that dog out of here," one social worker demanded as she raced back out the still-open door into the hallway.

Jamaica had her hand on Guinness's collar and was dragging him after the terrified woman, who was headed back outside. "Jamaica, put Guinness in the bathroom," I said, then reassured the social worker: the dog was very friendly and would never bite or even growl at anyone, but I'd make sure he stayed in the bathroom and didn't come near her.

Jamaica was doubled over. She threw herself down and began to roll on the floor, laughing, pointing her finger at the worker. Guinness was becoming increasingly playful, licking Jamaica as she rolled over and over. Jamaica continued to laugh, holding her stomach as she shouted, "You be scared of a friendly ol dog—you be a real fraidy cat." Jamaica would not budge from the floor, nor would she let go of Guinness, whom she was pulling along the floor toward the terrified woman in the hallway. I got the dog by the collar and righted the convulsed and breathless Jamaica, then put the dog in the bathroom. The social worker who had remained in the room went out to retrieve her terrified friend, and soon I heard good-natured laughter. As they came back in, one exclaimed, "That child can get a commotion going in nothing flat." I replied that she seemed to have a special talent for commotions—and I raced across the room to grab Jamaica, who was inching on tiptoe toward the bathroom door to let Guinness out again.

"You stay here, Auntie. I be showin them the whole house."

"Don't be so bossy, Jamaica," one of the workers said. "This isn't your house."

"That's okay," I replied. "Jamaica has been coming here for a long time—she can show you where everything is. I'll stay here, and if you have any questions just ask me or send Jamaica to get me."

As they walked down the hallway toward the back of the house, Jamaica exclaimed, "I have places here for jus my things. I'll show you where I keep my jewelry, money, an stuff in the piano chair. No one, not even you or the kids in the house, be touchin my stuff. It always be here an it better be or someone get they booty in big trouble."

In less than five minutes, Jamaica and her entourage returned to the kitchen. Miss Cortez, the taller of the two, said that everything seemed fine but that she had one question. Jamaica had told staff and kids at the school that she had gone to a dance with my teenage son, Ben.

My heart stopped. "Jamaica has never gone anywhere with my son. She goes nowhere when she comes to visit with anyone but me. I'm the one responsible for her, so I am with her at all times."

The thought that I could have caused trouble for my son sickened me. When the crack crisis was at its peak and newspapers showed children sleeping in police stations awaiting placement, a close friend had contemplated becoming an emergency foster parent for children in crisis, taking in children who were in dire straits for twenty-four to forty-eight hours while more permanent placements were arranged for them. But she did not follow up on this plan: colleagues in the child welfare field told her that children under this kind of stress have not infrequently accused temporary foster families of one kind of abuse or another. "I don't want to see my son being hauled off in handcuffs," my friend said. Though I had not seen any signs that Jamaica would make false accusations of me, I had been unceasingly vigilant in trying to avoid any circumstance that would subject anyone in my family to that danger. Suddenly I was fearful that I had failed and that that was the reason for this unexpected and untimely visit.

"Jamaica did come here one weekend last spring when Ben and some friends were going to their junior prom. She loved seeing everyone all dressed up in gowns and tuxedos for the prom. In fact, she took it upon herself to greet everyone at the door, and then she stood on the steps waving when they all left. Maybe she pretended she went, too. We have some pictures that Jamaica wanted me to take of her standing on the steps in the middle of all the teenagers as they were leaving. Would you like to see them?"

Before Miss Cortez could finish saying that this would not be necessary, Jamaica had flown into the study, where her photograph album was kept, and was returning with the album already open to the right page. "This be Ben an this be his fren Mark, an these be they girlfrens." She turned the page. "This be me wavin to them when they get in that big black car. See these flowers— the boys give the girls these flowers an the girls put them on they arms. See here, Ben an his fren give this flower to me, an the girls puts it in my hair."

Jamaica pointed to a picture of herself and the four teenagers. She was standing in the middle, between the tuxedoed Ben and his date, who wore a long, pale pink satin sheath gown. Jamaica was wearing a large turquoise shirt that hung down over yellow plaid pants. She was smiling and pointing to a yellow rose that the girls had pinned in the front of her hair.

"I see there are no problems here," Miss Cortez said. She gave me a paper to sign, which stated that she had been here on this date and had inspected my house. "Would you like to have Jamaica delivered to you by the van when we bring kids to the city?"

Before I had a chance to answer, Jamaica shouted, "No way—I ain't comin in again on no van. It make me sick to my stomach wobblin around in the back with all those stinky kids. I be comin in with Auntie in her car listenin to my music in peace."

"I think we'll stick with me picking Jamaica up—we have fun on our car rides into the city."

Jamaica was still shaking her head. "No, I jus won't be comin again on that ol van, no way, all that slippin an slidin. The way that lady drive make me sick to my stomach, lucky I din't puke. Auntie be pickin me up in my car—she be a better driver."

I stood at the top of the stairs while Jamaica walked down the sidewalk to the van. She jumped up and down at the window, shouting to the children inside. As the van pulled away, she stood waving, then began to run alongside it on the sidewalk until it turned the corner onto the avenue. Jamaica skipped back up the street, came up the steps and we went into the house.

She was sitting at the table when I told her we were going to visit Miss Pope at the copy store tomorrow. For a moment Jamaica was absolutely silent. She stared at me and then she stood up from her chair, walked to the closet, took out her jacket, and said, "Less go."

I told her we could not go to visit Miss Pope until tomorrow afternoon, she was expecting us after lunch.

Jamaica was quiet again, then she said, "Less go up to the store—I have to buy me a suit. Miss Pope like children to be dressed nice, an I don't have me a suit like she used to put on me. She won't like to be seein me in these raggedy ol clothes, like I be some kind of ol bum." Jamaica stood shaking her head. "I don't want to be lookin all ugly when I see Grandma."

I agreed with Jamaica that it would be nice for her to have something that she felt pretty in, and after an incessant barrage of "Less go now," we finally set off for Macy's.

"I be here before," Jamaica told me when we got off the bus. She pointed to a pizza place on Thirty-fourth Street and said, "Thas where I be eatin pizza with my mother. Can I get some of that pizza? It was good—my mother get it with pepperonis, an we eat first the little pepperonis, then the whole pizza."

Jamaica held my hand as we walked toward the pizza place. When we were inside, she looked around slowly, taking in the whole pizza parlor before exclaiming, "Yep, this be the place. My mother an me sit up on those high green chairs around that little table."

Jamaica pointed to some high stools around a countertop. She let go of my hand and raced over to climb onto one of the stools.

"You get the pizza, get pepperonis, an I sit here guardin these chairs so no one else be takin them—thas what I do when my mother go get the pizza for us."

Jamaica sat in the chair, looking around the room. Whether correctly or not she felt she had found a place that had once belonged to her and her mother. When I went to the counter to get the pizza, Jamaica sat looking around, talking to herself, recounting and reliving how she and her mother had eaten pizza here together, Bunny seemed alive—and, for the moment, she seemed to Jamaica to be within her grasp.

By the time I returned with two slices of pepperoni pizza, Jamaica had covered the round countertop with napkins to make a tablecloth. She sat, eating off the pepperoni piece by piece, taking tiny bites, small nibbles, until all of it was gone. Then she began to take all the cheese off the pizza slice, eating every strand, small bite by small bite. Next, she used her index finger to take off the tomato sauce, licking her finger after each scoop. When the pizza had been dismantled so that all that remained was a slightly red-smudged triangle of baked dough, Jamaica slid down off the stool and took the remainder of the slice to the garbage. "Thas the way me an my mother eat pizza," she said with finality. When she looked around the restaurant one final time before we left, I knew whom she was searching for.

"I be knowin exactly what I want," Jamaica told me as we rode up the escalator looking out over the handbags and perfumes of Macy's first floor. "I be gettin a suit—one of those suits with a skirt an a jacket like Grandma and Betty be wearin to church. You think they have that in this store? I don't be wantin to get any of those fancy dresses with ties in the back. I want me a suit— I know jus the kind I'm gettin."

Jamaica raced ahead. She walked right up to the saleswoman in the children's clothing department and asked, "Where the kids' suits at?"

The saleswoman didn't answer right away. She looked around to see who Jamaica was with, and when she didn't see anyone likely she asked, "Are you here by yourself?"

Jamaica pointed me out. "She be buyin me my suit."

It took Jamaica less than a minute to flip through sizes 8 to 10 before she pulled out a deep-purple suit with large black buttons.

"This be my suit," she said. "I be lovin purple, an it be Grandma favorite color. Less jus buy this."

Jamaica would not entertain other suggestions—she had found her suit and nothing else interested her, not even trying it on. When I insisted that she had to see if it fit, she threw on the jacket, pulled up the skirt, and, without zippering it, said, "It fits—less go."

"But you'll need shoes and a blouse."

"I got me shoes. I stuff em in my bag, but less get a pretty blouse like pink or yellow or somethin, but not white or green."

Slowly we leafed through the blouses until we came to a silky pale pink one with pearl buttons.

"That be beautiful wit my suit," Jamaica exclaimed. "An it feel good, too—soft and smoothy."

I agreed. We bought the suit and blouse and headed down the escalator. Jamaica, holding my hand, suddenly started to pull me back up the escalator.

"Less go back an put on my new suit, then we go back to the pizza place an look for my mother. If she there, she be seein me all beautiful in my new suit an she be sayin to me, 'Aren't you somethin wit you bad self.' "

I told Jamaica we had to get going—it was late, and everyone would be waiting for us to come home for dinner.

We did stop by the pizza place one final time, just to make sure.

The next morning seemed endless to Jamaica. She rode the bike we had brought back for her from the beach around and around the block, each time stopping by the stoop where I sat reading the paper and watching her. Finally it was time to get ready for the visit to Miss Pope. Jamaica put on her new suit, smoothing the front of the skirt, looking in the mirror. She posed at different angles—her head thrown back, her hands on her hips, her back to the mirror while she looked over her shoulder. Pleased with what she saw, she proclaimed, "This suit be lookin fine. Auntie, you better braid my hair."

"I don't know how to braid your hair."

"What you mean? Everyone be knowin how to braid hair. I kin braid your hair."

"I don't," I confessed. "I don't know how to make all those neat little braids like Staff does to your hair."

"And like Grandma do. Grandma be really mad if I be showin up at her house wit my fine suit on an my hair all ugly and natty like this. You better try to braid my hair—I show you how."

Jamaica and I struggled to draw her short, tight hair into neat braids that fitted close to her scalp. None of them held, nor could I manage any semblance of symmetry in the patches of hair I tried to torture into plaits. Despite my repeated failures, Jamaica remained hopeful with each attempt, until finally she looked in the mirror one last time and decided, "This be sad, this be a real mess. I need to git me a hat—you got one of them church-goin hats?"

I looked around and found a purple velvet beret, just the right color. It fit.

Jamaica ran to the piano bench, took out her jewelry, sorted through, and chose a small pin, a mother bluebird feeding two babies on the nest. She carefully fastened the pin on the hat, then looked in the mirror, twisting and turning the hat until the pin was slightly left of center. The beret was the perfect finishing touch—soft, glamorous, and completely covering up the failed braids. Jamaica was pleased. She twirled around in front of the mirror, her white lace legs and smooth black patent leather shoes whizzing in reflection as she assessed herself: "I be lookin fine in this suit."

Jamaica looked beautiful.

"I can put you lipstick on, Auntie?"

"No lipstick."

I took two pictures of Jamaica, one of her standing by the fire-place, the other as she looked at herself in the mirror.

"Auntie, you have pictures of me when I wuz a baby?"

"I don't, Jamaica, because I didn't know you when you were a baby."

"You know what I look like when I wuz little?"

"Not for sure, because I didn't see you then, but I think you must have been very small, with nice big brown eyes and a big smile. I bet you made lots of cute baby noises and were really fast at baby crawling."

"I remember what I look like when I wuz a baby, so when I see a picture of me, I just be grabbin it an givin it to us to put in my book. Maybe Grandma have a picture of me when I wuz a baby—she be knowin me longer than you. I think she got some pictures of me she give us for our pictures book. I know how my mother look so good I don't even need no picture of her. I can jus be drawin a picture of my mother if I want to—I see her face inside my eyes. I hope Miss Pope be bringin some of the pictures she take when I wuz at her house—them be my baby pictures."

We had just turned onto the Belt Parkway when Jamaica spoke. "Auntie, I decided somethin. I be comin to live wit you soon—you be my foster mother, like Miss Pope wuz. I go to that school near you house."

I looked over across the seat. Jamaica was looking directly at me, her hands folded in the lap of her purple suit, her velvet beret cocked to one side on her brown hair. "You know, Jamaica, if I was going to take any foster child, I would take you. But I've told you before, I don't plan to take a foster child. I can be your friend and your aunt and we can do lots of things together. I hope we will know each other for a long time, but you can't live with me. A kid your age needs someone at home. No one is in our house during the week to take care of you—everyone is at work or school. There is no one to watch over you."

"Thas okay, Auntie—you know I be takin care of myself for a long time when I wuz little. I don't need no grown-ups around. I got me plans about what I will do when I comes to live wit you. You'll get me my key made an put it on a little string for my neck. I'll walk home from that school near you house, let myself in, make me some food, an do my homework. Guinness will be there, glad to see me and all—he bark if any mens come to hurt me. I can take him for his walk and then jus wait till you come home. I could even do stuff to help you out, like set out the dishes and put up the rice for us to eat."

Jamaica continued to look directly at me. I kept my eyes on the road as much to avoid her stare as to avoid an accident. Jamaica was silent as we drove into Brooklyn. I drove on, saying nothing, listening to the soft reggae music, aware of an unbreachable gulf. I could not tell Jamaica my hopes and fears that we were on our way to what I thought might once again become the home she so desperately wanted and needed. I could not tell her that what she hoped for might still never come to pass. Jamaica needed the home she did not have—she needed to belong to someone.

Chapter 20

The copy store was at the end of a small strip mall in Flat-bush, Brooklyn. When we pulled up in front, two little boys—they looked to be about three or four years old—looked up from the sidewalk, where they were drawing flowers and happy faces with colored chalk. The smaller, a dark-skinned child with pierc-ing brown eyes and a mop of soft curls, saw us in the car and raced into the copy store. His companion, who had the same ebony skin, looked up from under a Knicks basketball cap. He continued to draw on the sidewalk until we got out of the car. When he saw where we were headed, he put down his chalk and followed a few feet behind.

In the copy store, several customers were working on self-service machines while a woman I assumed was Miss Pope worked on a large copy machine at the rear of the store. By this time, the smaller boy had raced to the back, pulled Miss Pope over, and was whispering into the hand he had cupped around her ear. The other child came into the store, scooted by us, and disappeared under the flap-over entrance to the other side of the counter. Now they both stood slightly behind Miss Pope, who had put down her work and was walking toward us.

Jamaica leaped up over the counter, catapulting herself over the Formica and springing up from a near somersault to the other side. She grabbed Miss Pope by the knees, hugging her. "Grandma, I be missin you for a long time."

Miss Pope picked her up, held her close, and said, "Well, I missed seeing your bad self, but you sure can cause people a lot of trouble. Here, child, let me look at you. You look pretty in that purple suit with that pretty hat on your head."

Jamaica had her arm around Miss Pope's neck and was leaning into her shoulder. "Thas you favorite color, right, Grandma?"

"You remember that—purple is my favorite color."

Miss Pope came over to the counter and nodded to me. She was about five foot ten and must have weighed 250 pounds. She was light skinned, nearly white, with dyed bright red hair, long dangling gold earrings, and a gold cap on her front tooth. She was dressed in a black skirt and fuchsia sweater, set off by a purple-and-gold belt around her midsection. Despite her ample weight, she had a sexy, rather glamorous appearance. As she walked toward me, I noticed she wore a high built-up shoe that caused her to list to one side. She introduced herself as Paulina Pope. "Just call me Lina—everyone does, except you, Jamaica. You call me Grandma, not Lina. Jamaica like to got it in her mind when she was small to call me Momma. I told her not to call me Momma because I was not her momma, she only had one momma and my kids only had one momma, so she should call me Grandma. Instead she took it in her head to call me Lina. I told her not to—only grown-ups call each other by their given names. Well, you know this child—she kept right on calling me Lina until I stopped answering, then she started to call me Grandma. You remember that, Jamaica?"

"Thas right, Lina," Jamaica replied, laughing as she ducked around behind Miss Pope's legs.

Miss Pope laughed, a hearty, deep-throated laugh, all the while shaking her head as she turned around and picked Jamaica up again. She held her close to her breasts. Jamaica rested her head on Miss Pope's shoulder. Miss Pope said, "I see you still are my bad little girl, a bit bigger now and a lot badder. What on earth are we going to do with you?" She hugged Jamaica tightly, then put her down.

"Who these, Grandma?" Jamaica asked, looking over at the children who stood close to Miss Pope. One boy stood slightly in back of her; the other was now sucking his thumb while holding tightly to a piece of Miss Pope's skirt.

"This is Darius," she said, looking down at the little boy at her skirt, "and this is Julio." She pointed to the other little boy, who stood quietly looking on. "Say hi, Julio. This is Jamaica—she used to live with me a while ago. Darius doesn't talk yet, but he will soon—right, Darius?"

Darius seemed to be about to cry. Miss Pope loosened his grip on her skirt and picked him up. "Don't you worry, honey—this lady is a friend of Jamaica. She is not here to take you away from me—I'm not going to let anyone take you away from me ever again."

She looked at me as she explained, "I took in Darius and Julio when a neighbor told me they were alone in their house. Someone had heard them crying. We got the super's keys and went in to get the kids. I knew their mother was on crack, so I called their grandmother. She said she would come to get them. Three days passed. She never showed up, but then their mother came back and took them with her. A week or so later, the same thing happened again. This time we called Child Welfare, who sent someone over to pick them up. They were taken away. Then I offered to keep them for a while and they came to me. Someone then said they should have a permanent foster home, because it did not look like their mother was going to straighten herself out anytime soon. Again someone came to get them with no notice at all—off they went. Both times it was a white worker who took them, so likely Darius thinks of that when he sees you. That place did not work out. Darius is a little backward—he doesn't talk and is still babyish. He has problems from a difficult birth which made him nearly deaf, so he is slow to speak. The foster home wanted to keep Julio but not Darius. Luckily the welfare had the good sense to keep the twins together. They called me again and I said I would take them only if I was approved as a permanent foster home. I couldn't stand for someone to come and snatch them up just when they were doing good. Last time it broke my heart, Darius screaming, crying, carrying on as he held on to me for dear life. Wasn't nothing I could do for him—I had no choice but to let them take him. I cried when they took them out. I was sick for weeks. Darius needs a lot of my attention. I don't mind giving it. He is such a sweet and frightened little thing. Julio looks out after his brother and helps Grandma. He's my little man, right, Julio?"

Julio nodded and smiled. He went over to take his brother by the hand and put his arm around him.

"These be living wit you, Grandma?"

"They are living with me, Jamaica."

"I hope they not be stayin in my room, playin wit all my toys and wearin my clothsis?"

"You know, Jamaica, I'll be real straight with you before we start anything. You did a bad thing to your grandma when you lied. You got me in trouble, you got Johnny in trouble, and you got yourself in even bigger trouble—it was you that got your own self sent away. Let's get that straight once and for all. You look right at me, child. I did not send you away. You caused all that trouble to yourself, and once you did it, wasn't nothing I could do. I could not help you anymore. It was like someone commits a crime, stealing or something, they get sent off to jail, and their mother or father can't help with the bad things that are going to happen to them."

"I wasn't stealin or nuthin bad like that, Grandma."

"I didn't say you were. All I mean is that you got yourself sent away from my house by the stories you made up, and now you don't have the nice home you had with Grandma anymore. *You* did that, do you understand that, child? *You did it.*"

"You know I wuz jus playin wit you, Grandma."

"That wasn't playing, Jamaica—that was lying, and you got us all in trouble."

Customers were beginning to come into the store. Miss Pope went back to finish her copy work and take new jobs in. Some were done quickly; otherwise the customer got a number to hand in when he or she came back to pick up the work. Darius and Julio went over to a corner of the room, where a play spot had been set up, and took out some toys. Jamaica went over to join them in play with a tea set.

I suggested something to eat. We decided on sweets from the bakery right in the mall. I offered to take all the kids so they could pick out what they wanted, but neither Darius nor Julio wanted to come. Jamaica raced out the door, eager to bring back coffee with milk and lots of sugar for Grandma.

"She love doughnuts wit jelly and coconuts," Jamaica told me as she picked out our treats.

Jamaica set out everything on a table near the back of the store and asked for my help in finding decorations so that the table would be like a party. I suggested she and the children draw on paper to make place mats. I would help them with the names. When everything was ready, Jamaica called Miss Pope.

"Auntie, you can go home witout me—I'm stayin wit Grandma tonight. I can stay wit you, right, Grandma? I be sleepin in you bed wit you, jus like we used to do. I don't need no bed or nuthin if these have my ol room."

"You can't stay with Grandma—I have you for the weekend," I said. "Remember what I told you? If you come to stay with me, you stay with me. You can't go off with somebody else. Besides, if I left you with Grandma when Hilltop did not give permission for you to visit her, we'd both be in trouble."

"Less not tell them—nobody be seein me wit Grandma, an you can pick me up an drive me back when the weekend over. That way they think I be wit you the whole time."

"That is also lying to Hilltop, and I can't do it. If you want to visit Grandma, let's ask her, and then we can tell Hilltop you're going to visit her. That way, you won't be lying and won't get yourself into trouble."

"Thas okay to you, Grandma?"

Miss Pope was quiet for a moment, then said, "I guess no harm will come. If your auntie wants to bring you after I'm through work on a Saturday, you can come have supper with us and stay over. No way I am going to have three of you here together in the store. A lot of people will be glad to see you, and so will the cat. You bring the suit you have on for Sunday so we can go to church. Pastor will be surprised to see your face."

Miss Pope turned to me. "You have to get written permission. If they say Jamaica can come, I'll be glad to have her. If not, there is no way I want her to come. I am not looking for more trouble because of this child. Now I have the chance of losing these two little ones, and I don't want that to happen to them or to me."

Jamaica nodded, excited at the possibility of revisiting Miss Pope's home.

I agreed to speak to the social worker at Hilltop and get in touch with Miss Pope before the next weekend. Thanksgiving was now a week and a half away. I hoped that if Jamaica spent the next weekend with Miss Pope and it went well, there still might be time for her to be invited for Thanksgiving.

The sky had grown dark by the time Jamaica and I left the copy store. It was quiet in the car as we drove back along the Belt Parkway. Jamaica looked out at the lights of the Verrazano Bridge. "I think I be goin back to live wit Grandma pretty soon. You know somethin, Auntie—she really mad at me, all right, but she still like me in her heart."

"I think you're right about that. I noticed it, too. I think your grandma still likes you in her heart."

Jamaica sat quietly in the dark, her eyes closed, her head tilted back. Without moving she said softly to herself, "Today I think she really do, an that make me feel soft in my heart, like music."

Chapter 21

About two o'clock on Monday, Miss Higby returned my call.

When I began to tell her about Miss Pope, she interrupted me: "I know all about Grandma—Jamaica ran in here before school to tell me she was going back to live with a Miss Pope. She was at my door grabbing at me before I had time to get to my desk. Is it true?"

"I did take her over to visit Miss Pope. She was Jamaica's foster mother after she was first found in the Port Authority." Miss Higby didn't know Jamaica's history from the case records: the Mercy reports had never been sent. What Hilltop had came from the group home, and the information was sketchy. Miss Higby knew only that Jamaica had no known relatives. The details of her placements were not consolidated in a single file anywhere—no one at Hilltop knew anything for certain about her actual past.

I told Miss Higby I hoped we could work together to reconcile Jamaica and Miss Pope. When I assured her that Miss Pope was black, though she looks as white as I am, she replied, "I hope you didn't take offense—you know that doesn't matter to me."

"I didn't take offense, but I am very aware that my race does matter to a lot of people, not the least of whom is Jamaica."

I told Miss Higby that, to judge by what I had seen on Saturday, there was a chance that Jamaica and Miss Pope could be reconciled. Clearly the relationship between them was not one-sided; Miss Pope cared about Jamaica in a way that might make a foster home placement still feasible.

"What would she want her back for? Jamaica caused her so much trouble."

"I don't know that she does want her back. All I know right now is that she will let Jamaica come for an overnight visit. I would like to arrange that, for this coming weekend. That's our start. Actually, right now I think Miss Pope would be horrified at the thought of taking her back—she caused her *too* much trouble. But she does like her, and that's the only thing we've got."

"What's your impression of Miss Pope? I can't go out there to inspect the home just for one overnight with no promise of anything permanent, and we can't let her be signed out to a stranger."

"All I can say about Miss Pope is that I trust her. She is lively, smart, and decent. She tried to get help for Jamaica rather than hiding the accusation Jamaica made—that showed real interest in the child. I see her with the two foster children placed there now. She is concerned, gentle, and good to them. I'd spend time with her myself—I like her. But she's not willing to go out on a limb, and I don't blame her. I'll have to sign Jamaica out to her house so there's a record that Hilltop knows and gives permission for her to be going there. I promised her I'd do that."

"How about this?" Miss Higby offered. "You sign her out first for your house, and right under it write in 'Saturday, Miss Pope,' and then list addresses for both of you. If you are so sure everything is on the up and up, I won't notice, you won't tell me, and Miss Pope will have it written down on paper. It will be filed quickly and disappear."

"Sounds good to me," I replied. "Short of fire or earthquake, Jamaica will be safe there."

"Just don't tell me more," Miss Higby said, "unless Miss Pope is interested in another trial at foster care. Then have her call me."

"What if she'll take her for Thanksgiving? Do you want her to call you for that? I can't sign her out to my house, because I won't be here."

"Let's just skip Thanksgiving—it's only a few days and she'll be fine here."

"It might be a good time for Jamaica to be with everyone in the family again," I added, taking Miss Higby into my strategy. "You know, we do want Miss Pope's family to get attached to her and think about her again."

"Yeah." Miss Higby laughed. "What they'll likely be thinking about is, 'When will this child be getting out of here and going back to Hilltop?' I'll go along with it if you can arrange it—at least it will be something for her. Let me know first if Miss Pope will be calling me, so I can get things rolling here. If she does take her for Thanksgiving and you are not signing her out to your house, I'll have to see a copy of her certification for foster care for the other two kids. Or," Miss Higby whispered, "maybe we can just say Jamaica has found her long-lost grandma."

"We're both beginning to sound and act like Jamaica." We had a good laugh together.

Miss Higby added, "Truth is, at times it's the only way, for her and for us."

I hung up and immediately called Miss Pope.

"Guess what—we're in luck. Hilltop says Jamaica can stay overnight this Saturday."

"I don't know if that means I'm in luck or my luck has run out. It's okay, she can come. When do you want to bring her?"

We planned to meet at the copy shop when Miss Pope closed it at six o'clock. "Make sure she brings that suit or has something else decent to wear. I take the children to church on Sunday, and

I don't want to be staying up all night making something presentable for her. When I first got Jamaica, all the clothing she had went right into the trash—that child had nothing but old hand-me-downs. When children are with me, they must look good."

I picked up Jamaica after school on Friday. When I went to pack her new purple suit so that she could wear it on Sunday, it was nowhere in sight. Nor was the purple hat, which she had worn back from New York.

I asked Jamaica where her suit was. She gave an indifferent shrug, the same shrug for the hat. I looked everywhere in her room, in her closets, in Tanika's closets.

Jamaica was no help. "Less go, less get our booties outta here."

"We need your suit. Grandma says you can stay over on Saturday. You need something nice for church."

"Grandma make it. She always be makin things for me to wear, she make it up real quick."

"Grandma is going to be tired after working all day. We have to get your suit. Let's go ask Staff."

"Don't be doin no good to ax Staff. Staff be stealin things for they own kids. I hear Staff say to other Staff when we get new clothis, that this size will fit her daughter, so she jus take it. That probably be where my suit go." Jamaica stood in her characteristic pose, hand on hip, head thrown back, glaring, shaking her head from side to side.

When I asked Staff if anyone knew what had happened to the new suit Jamaica had brought back less than a week ago, Staff knew nothing about it. She said, "These kids don't hold on to nothing—likely Jamaica gave it to someone to wear and don't want to say so."

Jamaica replied, "You be lyin—I put my suit in my closet, and now it be gone."

"All these kids steal," Staff offered.

I asked Staff if she would help us by looking in some of the other kids' closets. At first she glared at me, then without a word got up, walked into room after room, flung open the doors for Jamaica and me to look, then slammed the doors each time we were through.

"You see," Jamaica admonished me after the futile search. "You be wastin my time."

"And mine, too," I heard the disgruntled Staff mumble.

"And mine three," I added with fury.

"I be goin off to live wit my grandma," Jamaica told Tanika as we were looking for some pajamas.

"You ever comin back here?" Tanika asked.

"Likely not—right, Auntie?"

"No, you'll be back Sunday. I'll be bringing you back. You're going to visit Grandma, not to stay there."

"Maybe I *will* stay, maybe she be sayin I can an then I will."

"She'll be back on Sunday, Tanika, don't worry. And we'll bring back a surprise for you. Right, Jamaica?"

Jamaica put her arm around Tanika. "I be knowin what you want—one of those colorin books with princesses and crowns and stuff, right?"

Tanika nodded as she helped Jamaica put her clothing into the duffel bag I had brought along.

When we got past the stone pillars and Jamaica opened her eyes, she said, "Less not go to you house, less go right to Grandma. You can leave me there an I be going wit Grandma and the kids to the store tomorrow. I be helping her with those little kids. I always used to go to work wit her too, so she won't mind if I come."

I told Jamaica I had talked to Grandma and that she wanted us to come after work. "Besides," I said, "if I take you there now, I won't get any chance to be with you, to sing for you and make you those fried sweet potatoes."

Jamaica rolled her eyes. "I be tellin you you singin is hopeless, but you sweet potatoes is good. When we goin to Grandma?"

"We'll go tomorrow when she closes the store at six. I'll drive you, Grandma, and the twins to her house, then I'll come back on Sunday to get you and drive you back to school."

"I'll be hidin from you—you won't find me, so I'll be stayin at Grandma's."

"I know how much you want to live with Grandma. But this is a visit, this is not staying. You can't pull any tricks on Sunday— you have to go back to Hilltop, or we all get into trouble. Will you promise me that you will come with me on Sunday, not hide or run away or do anything that will cause trouble? If you do any of those things, I can promise you will not be going to Grandma's again. You got her into a lot of trouble once; she will not want you around if you do it twice. That will be the end with you and Grandma, and I won't be able to do anything about it. This is up to you, Jamaica."

Jamaica laughed. "You be lookin real serious, Auntie. You face look all funny an scrunch up—you be afraid or somethin?"

"I'm trying to help you with your grandma—that's why I'm taking you there. But I can't help you if you are bad and get your own self into trouble. I know you want to be able to go to your grandma again after this weekend. If you cause her trouble, that will be it—she won't let you come anymore."

"Auntie, don't you worry no more—I'm going to be so good, goody good good. I be good at night, good in the days, good in the house, good in the store. I only be good all the times."

With that Jamaica held her head up high and with exaggerated shoulder movements pretended to fly.

"A little angel behavior wouldn't hurt your cause, Jamaica."

She flapped her arms and doubled over in laughter.

Chapter **22**

Jamaica and I had planned to go to Coney Island the next time she came. All through the fall, kids had returned to Hilltop with news of the Cyclone and the Umbrella Twist, and Jamaica wanted to try both. Coney Island rides were still open on the weekends. I told Jamaica we could go if the day was warm enough.

"I hear they be scary, real scary, an that they make you sick enough to puke. All my frens say they great."

I knew it would be a long day, waiting to go to Miss Pope's house, so Coney Island seemed to be a good idea. First, though, we had to get some clothing for Sunday. We got up early and headed for Fourteenth Street, the south side of which is lined with children's clothing stores from Fifth Avenue to Seventh. Jamaica ran ahead of me. By the time I caught up with her, she was putting hot sauce on the skewered meat she had just bought from a street vendor. She stood with her hand out, waiting for me to catch up and pay.

"Next time, ask me first—what if I didn't have any money?"

"You always be havin money. I knew you did."

Jamaica was already looking toward the sweet smell of roasting nuts when I told her that she had to ask if she wanted something, not just grab it and then expect me to pay.

"What about them nuts—I can have thems after I finish my meat?"

The odor pulled my eyes to a silver cart where a vendor shoveled small scoops of honeyed nuts into paper cones. Jamaica watched him work, eager to finish her meat and begin the second course of this feast.

"How about after we buy your dress, so when you try clothes on they won't get sticky?"

Jamaica raced over to the vendor, the meat dripping hot sauce on her head as she held the wooden skewer aloft the way I had taught her to do with lollipops when she ran. "It's okay," she announced upon return. "He be here all afternoon in jus this spot."

Jamaica bought another purple outfit—this time a short purple flared skirt, purple tights, and a purple satin blouse with white pearl buttons. "Grandma be braidin my hair, so I won't be needin no hat this time," she said, glaring at me to make her point. "Grandma love purple, it be her favorite color."

I asked if she had a favorite color. She simply shook her head, looking at me in disbelief at my stupidity. Was there any other color for Jamaica but Grandma's favorite?

On the walk back home, Jamaica carefully ate one nut at a time, licking her fingers after each delicious taste. She wanted to give me some too, insisting that I bend over so that she could put it directly in my mouth. "I like feedin you, it's like you be my little baby. You can lick my fingers if you want. Tanika an me lick each other fingers."

I thanked her for her nuts but declined the finger-licking.

Back at home, Jamaica began preparations for Grandma's house. We laid out her clean clothes carefully and packed everything in a small suitcase. Jamaica rushed into the bathroom and returned with a can of jasmine body powder. "How about we sprinkle this all over my clothis, so that when I puts them on I be smellin all sweet an nice."

I told her that wasn't a good idea, that powder is not to put on your clothes but right on your body after you take a bath or shower. If you put it on your clothes, I told her, it would fall off and get all over everything, making a trail of white on the floor, the rug, the couch. I gave her the powder so that she could use it after she took a bath. I told her to only use a little at a time, so it wouldn't fall off.

"How about in my pockets?" she asked. "Then I be smellin good wherever I go, and it not be fallin out all over everything."

"If you want something in your pocket that smells good, you can spray a little perfume on a handkerchief and keep it in your pocket. Let's do that—then you'll have the nice smell you want, and you won't get powder over everything you put in your pocket."

Jamaica and I found a small lace handkerchief. I watched her carefully spray it with my Chanel, then fold it into a little square. She held it up to her nose, closed her eyes, and breathed in the scent. "Grandma be sayin when she near me, 'This be one sweet-smellin child. I loves the smell of this bad little girl.' "

Just as we were walking out the door, Jamaica turned around and ran back inside. She went straight to the piano bench and in one move scooped and dumped all her possessions onto the floor. She sorted through her jewels, throwing rings, plastic beads, bracelets, and pins to the side, until she found the rhine-stone necklace I had given her for dressing up. She continued to dig through for the matching rhinestone earrings. She bunched them all together in her fist and slipped them into her pocket.

"Okay, less go," she announced, walking away from the mess on the floor.

"First, let's put everything back," I said, for what seemed to me the thousandth time. Glaring, Jamaica complied.

"Are you going to wear your jewels with your new purple out-fit?"

Again the glare, signifying "You must be crazy," followed by eyebrow-raising, head-cocking, and tongue-clucking to signify disbelief.

"These be for Grandma, these be her present. My grandma loves jewelry, but she say don't let anyone give you that fake gold, only really gold. I don't have no really gold, cause all you give me was those fakey gold things, so I have to give Grandma these sparkly jewels. She love them, an when she go out she put them on an she say, 'I have these beautiful jewels an such because of that bad little girl Jamaica—she give them to me.' Grandma be all smilin and happy wit me.

"I think I be puttin Grandma's present in my suitcase, or you could carry it for me in you bag. I wouldn't want to be losin them when I go on those rides. If I lost the jewels, I be really sad because then Grandma might not say how happy she be."

"I think Grandma would be happy to see you, just to see that bad little face of yours, even if you had no jewels to give her."

"Maybe it be true," Jamaica said as she handed me the jewels for safekeeping. She closed her eyes and said, "I be makin a wish right now, but I better not tell you. Tanika say wishes don't come true if you tell. I be wishin Grandma love me an want me to live wit her. Auntie, you close you eyes an wish it wit me, that make two wishes together."

Jamaica and I held hands, closed our eyes, and together wished that Grandma would want Jamaica to live with her forever.

Chapter 23

By noon we were whizzing along the Belt Parkway, listening to Jamaica's latest favorite singer, Gloria Gaynor. We had our day planned. First Nathan's for hot dogs and French fries, and then the rides. I tried to warn Jamaica that she might not be able to go on some of the rides without an adult. I told her that under no circumstances would I go on the Cyclone or the Umbrella Twist—they would make me dizzy and sick to my stomach. She could count on me for the merry-go-round, the Ferris wheel, and the bumper cars. That was it. Each time I announced this, Jamaica pointed in my direction, laughed hysterically, and chanted, "You be chicken! *Bawk bawk bawk,*" clucking with delight at what she perceived as my fear and frailty.

Jamaica wanted rides first, food later, so we headed directly for the Cyclone. She pulled me faster than I wanted to walk. The late fall day was warm. The high, bright sun threw the shadows of the roller coaster and the moving cars onto the surrounding dirt. We stood for a while underneath the twisting and turning structure, listening to the clanging as chains pulled the roller-coaster cars to the ascent. Moments of breath-holding silence were followed by the terrified and excited screams that rode along with the passengers to the bottom of the hill. Jamaica held my hand and her breath as the cars climbed the hill. When the brake released the car into its downward plunge, Jamaica leaped into the air, screamed, clapped, and punctuated her excited dance with a series of "Yes"es exclaimed and held on to like a long loud hiss.

"Okay, Auntie, I be goin now—give me my money."

"I don't think you can go alone. I don't see kids your age. Let's go read the sign."

The sign said, "No one under eighteen allowed unless accompanied by an adult."

"Then you be comin wit me." Jamaica pulled me toward the cashier's booth.

"I'm not going on the Cyclone—I told you I wouldn't, and I won't."

Jamaica pulled even harder. "You jus be ol, an ol white chicken—you jus be afraid." She stomped off toward the cashier and tried to buy a ticket, then ran back toward me and tried to butt her head into my stomach. I picked up her flailing body and, holding her wrists tightly, sat her down on the bench in the shadow of the Cyclone. Reason could not match Jamaica's disappointed desire. She continued to flail and scream, "You no good to me, you no good to me at all—less jus go on to Grandma house."

My suggestion that we find some rides she *could* go on fell on deaf ears. Jamaica refused to move, and even when she quieted down she sat listless, her angry glare the only exchange between us. "I'm not goin on nuthin if I can't go on this," Jamaica announced. "Wake me up when it time to go to Grandma house—she let me do stuff when I be wit her." With that Jamaica put her head on my lap, pulled her legs up underneath her on the bench, and closed her eyes. I stroked her head as she dozed off in the sun.

I felt exhausted. I sat watching the roller coaster go up, plunge down, climb a series of increasingly steep inclines, plunge again, until the highest ascent and plunge were reached. The volley of screams increased with the height of the incline, until the descent from the highest brought forth a wave of screams that lingered in the air after the laughing passengers returned to the platform, undid their safety belts, and left the cars. I noticed that one young woman remained on the car each time it discharged its passengers. She sat waiting for the car to be loaded again, gave the attendant her ticket, and stayed for another ride. When she got to the ascent each time, she waved to a woman who sat reading a Bible on the bench across from us. She never screamed. The woman on the bench had uncanny timing: she would stand up and wave exactly when the car was at the highest ascent, sit down, and read her Bible again, only to stand and wave when the car arrived again at the ascent.

She saw me watching her. She had also been watching us. She closed her Bible and came over. "That's my daughter. She'll be getting off soon—her money is about to run out. Every Saturday she comes here and rides over and over again until all her money is gone. She's been here now for nearly two hours. That child loves this roller coaster. Often, at this time of year, the attendant lets her ride free for all afternoon depending on the crowd, but that's not likely today—they're too busy."

She interrupted herself to wave, then continued: "If you want her to take on this little one, I'm sure she'll be glad to do it for the price of a ticket. I couldn't keep her in school when she was younger. She would always sneak out here and beg for rides. I started to come with her. That was the only way I could get her to go to school—to promise her that I would bring her on Saturdays when I don't work and that I would wave to her each time she got to the top."

The sleeping Jamaica popped up. "I can go wit her, Auntie?"

"How old is your daughter?" I asked the woman. She was watching the roller coaster take on new riders; with straw hat in hand, she awaited the moment when the roller coaster would arrive at the top, her daughter would look down, and she would wave again.

"Nineteen yesterday," she replied.

"Well, Jamaica, looks like we found us a roller-coaster-riding baby-sitter with probably more experience in roller-coaster riding than anyone we'll ever meet. We can ask her when she gets off."

Jamaica raced up to the rail. She stood by shyly, watching and hoping that one of the exiting breathless roller-coaster riders would be her baby-sitter.

Finally, after a few more rides, a young woman dressed in a long white robe, with a white scarf tied around her head, rose from the wooden seat, flipped back the metal safety bar, undid her belt, and walked toward her mother, who stood next to us.

Her mother quickly summed up the situation. "This child wants to go on the coaster, this lady don't, so I said you might take her for the price of a ticket."

The young girl spoke softly. She had a round, unmade-up face. She approached the matter as one would a business deal. "How many times you want to ride?"

"Three," Jamaica replied. "Okay, Auntie?"

The baby-sitter nodded. I could see that Jamaica had struck an acceptable deal, so I readily agreed.

"More if she wants?" the young woman questioned, her eyes fixed on me from behind small gold-rimmed glasses.

"Maybe a couple more. We'll have to see—I don't want her to get sick."

"She won't get sick," the seasoned traveler assured.

"I won't be scared, either," said Jamaica with bravado.

We bought six tickets. I watched the attendant buckle Jamaica in beside the young woman, whose name was Kisha. "Wave to me, Auntie!" she called over her shoulder, holding her hands up over her head to defy the instruction I had given her to hold on tight.

I listened to the clackety-clack as the chain pulled Jamaica to the top of the ride. Her hands were now on the bar and her head was bowed. At the top, there was no bravado, no look back for a wave. Kisha and her mother waved as usual. Jamaica could not be seen. I imagined she had crouched down. I feared she might have dived to the floor, sliding out of her seat belt on the way. I questioned my judgment in letting this happen and hoped that Kisha had more good sense than one might hope for from someone whose main goal in life appeared to be endless rides on the Cyclone. I had the sickening thought that I never would have let my own children go. The wait seemed interminable, the screams a haze around the numbing fear I felt for Jamaica's safety. I wanted to see her back on the ground. Perhaps I had given in to Jamaica's need to master fear and terror by ignoring real dangers. I wished I had never let her go.

When the car came rumbling in to discharge its passengers, Jamaica was the first one off. She ran over to me and exclaimed, "Less get our booties outta here—that ride make me sick to my stomach."

Kisha was glad to have four more tickets, and Jamaica was eager to get away from the Cyclone as fast as she could. "Feel my heart, Auntie," she said, placing my hand on her skinny chest.

"Your heart is beating so loud and fast, Tanika can hear it at Hilltop."

"You know how some peoples faints in church, jus falls out on the floor. I be thinkin I wuz gonna jus fall out so I hold on to Kisha. She be smilin wit her eyes closed and talkin to herself and all, an I be so scared I jus go low in my seat an hol on an not look when I go up, cause then I know I be comin right back down. I wuz thinkin I be dead like that ol man my mother an me drag down the stairs. Then my stomach go bloop, and I starts thinkin I'm gonna puke all over Kisha white clothis. That make her mad, and then she be pushin me right out the seat."

We left the shadow of the Cyclone, the noisy clatter of the climbing chains, the terrified and excited screams, and headed off in the bright fall sun down the boardwalk toward Nathan's. "I think I was wrong to let you go," I told Jamaica as we walked along holding hands.

"I made you let me go cause I be buggin you and buggin you."

"You didn't make me let you go. I let you go because I wanted you to have fun doing the thing you wanted to do so much, but sometimes what you want is not good for you and I have to tell you so. Just like watching those scary movies like *Friday the Thirteenth* and all those Chucky movies is not good for you, so I don't let you watch them. I think this was too scary for you. I should not have let you do it, and I'm sorry I did."

"Thas because you be chicken," Jamaica said flying down the boardwalk flapping her wings with a loud "*Bawk, bawk, bawk.*"

In this case, I thought, maybe I *was* chicken. I ran down the boardwalk after Jamaica, flapping my wings and shouting, "*Bawk, bawk, bawk.*"

Jamaica ran faster, her head turned over her shoulder as she screamed into the air, "*Bawk, bawk, bawk.*"

I ran faster, too. We *Bawk-bawk-bawked*, all the way to Nathan's Hot Dogs.

Chapter 24

At about five o'clock we headed back to the car and set out along the Belt Parkway for the long-awaited rendezvous at the copy store. This time Jamaica did not put on her tapes. We rode along; she dozed, her chin falling slightly over her rising and falling chest.

"You gonna be missin me when I be at Grandma's house?" she asked.

"I *will* miss you, Slippery Shoes," I told her. "I like when you visit me and we do things together. Who will I make French toast with tomorrow, who will I tell not to pour the whole bottle of syrup on their plate, and who will I sing for?

"You going to miss me?" I asked.

Jamaica rolled her eyes, shook her head no, and asked, "You be pickin me up, right?"

"I'll pick you up about three o'clock and drive you back."

"We be gettin my Kentucky Fried?"

"We'll ask your grandma if there is a Kentucky Fried near her house. If there is, we'll stop there. If not, I'll stop at our usual place on Fourteenth Street and bring it with me: half a bucket, mashed, gravy, biscuits, and honey."

"Maybe I bring some food from Grandma house—she make

the best food they is. I learn a new song at Hilltop. We be havin a big play at school for Thanksgivin. Me, Tanika, an some ol girls be in this group, all the kids who sing good. Mr. T. Jones, he be a ol fat black man—he sing good, though. He teach us this song an some good moves while we sing. I'm gonna sing this song for Grandma. She love singin, she sing on the radio when she wuz young, and she have one fine voice. She sing in church and everyone love to hear my grandma singin. I hope I be goin to church wit her tomorrow an we all be singin together. I know some of those church songs when I live wit Grandma before."

Jamaica closed her eyes and began to sing in her low, clear voice, recalling and imagining herself where she wanted to be, in church singing with her grandma. At first she sang the song straight through, humming over the words she did not know, moving back in when she did.

"What a fren we have in Jesus, all our sins and griefs to bear. / What a priv a lidge to care ree ever ee thing to God in prayers. / Can we find a fren so faithful, is there trouble any where, / Jesus know our ever ee weakness, take it to the Lord in prayer."

After one time through, she picked up the beat, swaying and clapping as she increased the volume and sang a whole new version, syncopated.

"How comes you never take me to church wit you?" Jamaica asked, interrupting herself.

"I don't go to church," I told her.

Jamaica shook her head. "Grandma say that be no good, peoples gots to go to church. I'm tellin Grandma that I goes to church every Sunday when I'm at Hilltop, but I can't be goin to church when I'm wit you cause you don't be goin and bringin me. Maybe I have to be wit Grandma on Sunday from now on, so that I can be goin to church like she want me to do."

We pulled into the mall and parked the car right outside the copy shop. Before the engine had stopped running, Jamaica was out the door and into the shop. I saw her race past Darius and

Julio and leap over the counter. Miss Pope picked her up and held her tightly as Jamaica wound her legs around Miss Pope's waist.

"*She*," Jamaica tattled, pointing in my direction, "let me go on the roller coaster, even though I wuz not supposed to, an I got all scared and sick to my stomach."

Jamaica shook her head and nestled further into Miss Pope's shoulder. Miss Pope looked at me over the glasses perched on her nose. I felt sheepish, caught in the act, the target of a clear accusation of, if not child abuse, at least child neglect.

Miss Pope held Jamaica away from her in straight-armed eye-to-eye view, shook a finger at her, and said, "There you go again, making bad accusations about the very people who are trying to do good for you. You apologize to your auntie for saying that. I won't have you in my house again, if you go on accusing people of things."

She put Jamaica down and brought her over to stand right in front of me.

"You tell your auntie you are sorry for saying bad things about her. You are one ungrateful child; you always were. I guess you'll never change. After all this woman has done for you, you come racing in here and the first thing you have to say to me is that someone who has been good to you did something bad to you. Maybe you should go right back where you came from. I don't like the kind of badmouthing of people you do—you are not to be trusted."

"It's okay," I told Miss Pope. "I told Jamaica I was wrong to let her go on the roller coaster. It really was too scary."

Miss Pope was angry. "It's not okay with me. This is the kind of thing this child does. The child has no loyalty or kindness in her heart. If she is going to be in my house, she has to stop this right now. I won't allow this kind of behavior against people who are nice to you: me, your aunt, my children, anyone else. Do you understand me?"

Jamaica stood in front of a head-shaking Miss Pope, who held her firmly by the shoulders. She pushed Jamaica away from her. "You apologize to your auntie for saying that. I won't have you in my house if you go on accusing people who are nice to you of doing bad things to you."

She brought Jamaica over to stand right in front of me. "You go ahead now and tell your auntie that you are sorry for acting in that nasty way to her."

Jamaica whispered a perfunctory "I'm sorry."

Miss Pope looked down at Darius and Julio, who had come over to stand by her. Darius had his hand around her leg. Miss Pope announced, "These two would never dream of saying bad things against me, it is not in their nature—right, children?"

Julio and Darius looked solemn as they slowly shook their heads up and down in agreement.

Jamaica stood to the side, picked up all the loose paper clips she could find, and made piles of them. Julio and Darius followed close behind Miss Pope while she closed the copy store, pulled down the steel safety shutter, and secured the big metal padlock. We all piled in my car and headed for her house nearby.

"I'm gonna sleep in my ol bed, Grandma?" Jamaica asked from the backseat, where she sat between Julio and Darius.

"No, it's now Julio's bed. Julio and Darius share your old room. You are going to sleep in the small room that used to be Betty's room. I put your old blankets and some of your old toys in that room. If you get lonely, though, you can take your blankets and pillow and sleep on the floor with the other kids."

"Not wit you, Grandma?"

"Not with me. I don't want any kids sleeping in my bed. If I let you, I have to let them, and I am too tired to be bothered by children's feet in my stomach."

Jamaica laughed. "I use to kick you when I be a baby an be sleepin wit you, Grandma?"

"You were one bad little sleeper. I always ended up with your elbow in my face or your foot in my stomach."

Jamaica laughed.

When we arrived in Miss Pope's neighborhood of two-story attached brick houses, Jamaica asked if she could direct me to Miss Pope's home. Miss Pope gave permission with a qualifying "Let's see if you remember."

With unvarying precision hampered only by her inability to know right from left, Jamaica guided me until we pulled up in front of the one house that had ceramic tubs of still-blooming pink impatiens on either side of the front door.

"I can still water your pretty flowers, Grandma?" Jamaica asked.

"They'll be needing a good watering, Jamaica. You can do it for me tomorrow."

Inside, the house was immaculate. Beige wall-to-wall carpeting covered the floors. Jamaica raced through the rooms, shouting as she ran, "You still have my old sofa, you still have my big ol green chair we be sittin in to watch TV. You still have my little rockin chair an table where I be doin my homework."

Miss Pope shook her head and smiled. "That child must have imagined I hit the Lotto and went out and bought all new furniture. I've had the same old stuff in this place for nearly twenty years."

"I think she's glad that some things stay the same."

Jamaica tried to sit on Miss Pope's lap. Miss Pope told her to go into the den and watch TV with the children. Jamaica left for a moment, then reappeared, peering around the doorjamb.

"You be makin any of my favorites, Grandma?"

"You wait and see, child—I know what you like," Miss Pope told her as she shooed her back into the den.

Jamaica shouted from down the hallway, "You go home now, Auntie—we'll be needin to eat soon."

Miss Pope shook her head. "She hasn't changed or sweetened one little bit. If anything, it looks to me like she is getting harder. One time she told me her mother would take me for a fool because I worked. She told me that her mother told her only fools had jobs and that you could get money lots of other ways but working. I straightened her out right quick, but I think at times she is just too far gone. Even now, she only likes this place for what it can give her. She is not like the other kids, and they had it pretty bad, too. She has no real feeling for me. She just wants to get herself back here. It's like there is no kind of love inside her. Love doesn't grow inside Jamaica; maybe it never will."

"Jamaica hasn't had much love herself," I said. "Did she ever mention to you that her mother had another baby before her? She says it's an older sister. I don't know if it's true or not; I don't know if a lot of what I have been told is true, but she told me that baby still lives with her grandmother and that when her mother got pregnant again, with her, her grandmother threw her mother out. If that's true, Jamaica has been homeless from her very beginnings. I can see why she wants to move back with you—it's very nice here."

Miss Pope poured us both a beer. She took me into her bedroom. The walls were lined with pictures of her family. A black-and-white photo of a handsome couple coming out of a small church in the trees stood in a gold frame on her bureau. "That was me when I married my husband at nineteen. He was twenty-one, worked as a Pullman car porter until his death. That's how we have this house—we always bought us a house of some kind, sold it, and bought us another." When I asked about the picture of her dressed in an evening gown and standing in front of a microphone, she said she had had a successful career as a singer and in this photo was accepting an award for a hit record. There were several more photos of her singing in clubs and behind the microphones at radio stations. Then she pointed to many family graduation pictures, of everyone from young kindergarten graduates to her daughter's graduating from college, and she showed me a scholarship letter to the private school her grandson attended. And there was Jamaica, dressed for church in a purple suit with matching straw hat and flowers, a miniature version of the suit and hat Miss Pope wore as she stood smiling beside her on a bright, sunny day outside the doorway of a large brick church.

"Does it hurt you that after all these months, you don't mean any more to her than some old fly to be swatted away when you irritate her? You know she is just waiting for you to get out of here."

"I know that, and the truth is that sometimes it bothers me a lot. I get hurt and disappointed at those times when it is so obvious how little I mean to her. When she has been really rough, I've thought, 'I'm getting out of here—I never want to see this kid again.' I calm myself down when I think of how little she really has, and eventually I get over it. I've thought it may even be wrong to take her to my house for weekends. You can't compare a Saturday trip to Coney Island to a home. Her visits with me only make her want more from me than I want to give her. Then I feel guilty and bad because I don't want to give her what she wants—a home and someone to care about her. You're the only hope she has for that."

Miss Pope nodded. "With her, you have to keep your sights set low. She will never be what my grandchildren are, or maybe what Julio and Darius can be helped to become. But if she doesn't have to go to jail or end up strung out on the streets, maybe that still might be something."

"Maybe she can do better than that, but you're right, that still would be a lot. She isn't headed for much now—I think a home here with you is the best and only shot she has at any kind of decent life."

Miss Pope sighed. She sipped her beer and smiled. "I think you are trying to sucker this old lady back into something."

"I know I am."

She gave me a warm hug. I put on my coat. When Miss Pope called, Jamaica came quickly, running past me into the kitchen, eager to help set the table.

"Say good-bye to your auntie," Miss Pope instructed a busy

Jamaica, who was bringing the step stool over to the cabinets where the plates were kept.

"Bye, Auntie," Jamaica parroted as she rooted through the closets. "Don't forget to ax Grandma about my Kentucky Fried!"

Miss Pope shook her head. "That's what I mean. I don't know if I want to be that person who will never be more than someone who is supposed to put something into that child's greedy little outstretched hand."

"I'll still take her on weekends if that would help."

"Let's see how things go around here," Miss Pope said. "Truth is, I'm in a bit of a financial pinch, with a second mortgage and all. I need to help out my children with their bills. I could use the money."

Jamaica did not come to the door to say good-bye to me. I didn't call her. I did not want Miss Pope's attention called to this slight.

I drove home in the dark, with no sound in the car. Jamaica was finally back with Miss Pope. I hoped that Jamaica would be on her best behavior and that Miss Pope needed the money an awful lot.

Chapter 25

When I arrived back at the house on Sunday, Jamaica, one of Miss Pope's granddaughters, and Julio were jumping rope out front. Jamaica ran up to the car and pounded on the window.

"I ain't hidin from you, Auntie, cause I be comin here for Turkey Day—Grandma say I can. You get me my Kentucky Fried?"

I got out of the car and picked her up. She twisted my hair around her finger until it pulled and hurt. When I put her down, she ran into the house. Miss Pope appeared, with Jamaica pretending to hide behind her, her skinny body nearly obscured by Miss Pope's large frame.

"Jamaica told me to tell you that she is not here," Miss Pope announced.

"I was afraid she would do this," I replied. "I told her she better not, because if she did, she would not be allowed to come back. Some little bird told me you said she could come for Thanksgiving. Too bad she had to do this and ruin her Thanksgiving plans."

Miss Pope just shook her head. "I don't know what I'm going to do with that child. She is so bad. I wanted her to be here with us for Thanksgiving, but now, I just don't know."

"Psyched—psyched you!" Jamaica screamed. She crouched down and pounced out in the middle between us. "Don't worry, Grandma, I be comin and I be eatin so much I get fat like you." She jumped up and wound her legs around Miss Pope's waist.

"Go get your things, Jamaica. Don't take your good clothes back. They'll only be stolen."

"I be comin back for sure, Grandma?"

"If I can help it, yes, but I can't say anything for sure."

When Jamaica was out of sight, Miss Pope spoke softly. "I am an old fool, but there is something about that child, mean and wicked as she can be, that touches me in my heart. Maybe it's just that she has absolutely nothing of her own, nothing she can hold on to. When I think of her clothes getting stolen, of how there is no one who cares to braid her hair, to make sure she is clean, smells good, is learning, I feel deeply for her. Then she turns around and is mean as a snake. Just today she made a comment to my daughter that maybe she would go live with her because I was old and would die first. She tries to grab everything at once, and when she does, she destroys what little she has."

Jamaica reappeared carrying a shopping bag and wearing one of Miss Pope's fancy hats. She sauntered down the steps, her hand on her hip, her head thrown back as she struck one sexy pose after another. Pretending that nothing unusual was going on, she opened the car door and began to get in.

"At least it is on her head and not in the bag," Miss Pope whispered.

"That's progress," I acknowledged as Miss Pope put out her hand to retrieve her hat from Jamaica's head.

"There were no problems. She did have nightmares—something about the Ku Klux Klan. What is she learning up there? She woke up crying and screaming about people with white sheets trying to break in and kill us. I did end up letting her sleep with me, but I told her to keep her mouth shut or they would be accusing me of abusing her and not let her come again. If you can arrange it, and find a way to get her here, I will take her for Thanksgiving."

I asked Miss Pope for a copy of her foster care certification. I wanted to make sure Hilltop had this so that a Thanksgiving visit was not stalled by bureaucracy. Miss Pope was concerned about losing the originals, so Jamaica and I drove to a shopping mall, copied them, and brought her papers back to her. Jamaica picked up Darius and patted Julio on the head. "I be you big sister," she told them with authority. "Don't you worry, I be comin back an we play copy store again—right, Grandma?"

Miss Pope put her hand on Jamaica's shoulder. "I want you back, child. I will try to make sure you come back for Thanksgiving, but I can't be sure. I might not have my say. Auntie and I will do our best to get you back here, I promise."

Jamaica shook her head and said, "You better."

As soon as we were in the car, Jamaica broke open the Kentucky Fried Chicken. She ignored the white plastic spoon and delicately dipped her forefinger into the mashed potatoes, coating each little scoop of mashed potatoes with a dip into the gravy. "You want to know how I know Grandma still like me?" she asked. "When we go to church she hole me by my hand and she be sayin to all her frens, 'Look who I have here—my little ol bad girl is back.' Her frens kiss me an all an say to Grandma, 'She be livin wit you again, Lina?' Grandma say, 'No, not yet, but I hope soon. You likely be seein her at Thanksgiving.'

"I think that mean Grandma like me, but not as much as she like Darius an Julio—they be her kids now, they be livin wit her for sure. I like Grandma house. She have things all pretty an she make so much bacon I can eat all I want."

"I know your Grandma still likes you," I said. "She told me so. I like you, too."

"But you don't want me to live wit you, right, Auntie?"

"If I wanted any kid to live with me, it would be you, but I don't want to take care of any kids, now that Samantha and Ben are grown. Children need someone to take care of them every single day."

"I don't," Jamaica said. "I be knowin how to take care of myself better than you likely know how to take care of youself. I can fight, use a knife, an run fas an hide. Don't matter, maybe I be livin wit Grandma again so I can't be goin to live wit you even if you want me.

"I loves this song we be singin at church. Grandma love it too, we be singin an movin back an forth. I wuz happy I knew the words an all from school. I sing loud like Mr. T. Jones teach me, sayin every word nice an clear, jus like he tell me to. Grandma look down at me, she smile an pat me on my back. 'You have one fine voice, Jamaica,' she tell me, so I jus go on singin an singin wit all the peoples an clappin an all. Don't sing wit me. You know you don't know how to sing good an I don't want my singin all scratchy an spoil."

Jamaica's voice filled the car. We drove into the twilight and headed back upstate to Hilltop. She sang, she hummed, she clapped, and I kept my scratchy ol voice to myself. Jamaica claimed the song and the moment.

> *Lean on me when you're not strong,*
> *I'll be your fren, I'll help you carry on.*
> *For I know, that it won't be long,*
> *till I'm gonna need somebody to lean on.*

Chapter 26

Over the phone, Miss Higby asked, "Is it true—is she going to live with her grandma?"

"Maybe, but first let's get her there for Thanksgiving. Miss Pope said she could come, and I have the foster care certification for the other two kids. I will fax it to you. Miss Pope said you should call her to make the arrangements. The house is beautiful, well kept, clean, the kids have their own beds, the neighborhood looks safe. Anything you need for a home visit checklist, I can provide. Miss Pope is a grandmotherly, hardworking, extremely nice woman. She is both strict and kind, perfect for Jamaica. Jamaica won't be able to put too much over on her. If life gets hard for us, we can both go and join her—it's nice there, and Jamaica recommends the food."

"Maybe I should give you part of my salary," Miss Higby joked.

"Okay, I'll take it. How much are you offering? If our scheming works, we hit the jackpot: Jamaica gets a home."

Miss Higby and Miss Pope made the plans. Jamaica was dropped off and picked up by the Hilltop van, with all the other children going places for Thanksgiving vacation.

The week after Thanksgiving, Miss Pope phoned. The visit

had gone very well. Jamaica was no problem to anyone. "The child was so happy to be here that anything I wanted her to do she did in a flash, and when she messed up I almost felt sorry for her—no child should have to be on such good behavior for fear of losing their home.

"Your sneaky plan worked," she told me with a laugh. "I've let Hilltop know I want to apply for foster care. They are sending someone out next week. I'd like to have Jamaica by Christmas."

"Should I get her next weekend and bring her out to visit?" I asked.

"She has to come here every weekend now. I've arranged it with Miss Higby. The van will bring her and pick her up." These visits were a necessary part of the preplacement workup for foster care. "We hope to get her into a school here right after Christmas vacation," Miss Pope concluded.

When I asked Miss Pope if I could take Jamaica overnight the third Saturday in December to bring her to Radio City as we had planned, she was hesitant. I heard the reluctance in her voice. Then she said, "I don't think that would be a good idea. I don't want her to be doing anything different from Darius and Julio. She'll be lording it over them, and it won't be fair. I think you better just let that go. Jamaica has to learn our ways now, fit in here with the others. For a while it will be best that she doesn't do anything special with you."

"How about if I just come over on Sunday and take her for a walk? I'd like to let her know why I won't be seeing her, so she won't just think I dropped her and forgot about her."

"Sunday is not good—we'll be at church, then we go to my son's house to eat. You know, it won't matter to Jamaica. That's the way she is. She'll forget all about you as soon as she knows she is going to be living here. I don't want to give her any opportunity to play you off against me or to feel that she's more special than the other two. I know that child. She'll be using you to make herself better than the others. Over Thanksgiving I heard her say something to the other kids about the jewelry she has at your house, about your dog and your garden, where she has her own tomato plant. She also told them that they have to stay home because you only want her with you—that you wouldn't like them, you only like her."

I was stunned and felt terrible. This turn of events was sudden and completely unexpected. With no warning or planning I had become completely free of Jamaica, and I didn't want to be. Nothing had prepared me to expect that Miss Pope would exclude me so swiftly from Jamaica's life. Jamaica and I had plans to keep. We had talked about what we would do over the Christmas holidays. Samantha promised Jamaica she could have the black velvet dress that had been hers when she was Jamaica's age, and that she could wear it when we all went to see *The Nutcracker.* I didn't like what was happening at all. It was as though Miss Pope's house had opened up and was beginning to swallow Jamaica. She was about to vanish.

I wanted to keep in touch with Jamaica, to see her occasionally, and, above all, not to be another person who was in her life for a while and then just vanished. I was glad to hear from Miss Pope that the things Jamaica had at my house meant something to her and that she held on to some personal experiences and memories. I didn't feel she should have to give them up.

Though Miss Pope and I had never actually discussed what would happen if Jamaica went to live with her, I had taken it for granted that I would continue to see her, at least for a while. I had felt that Miss Pope wanted that, too, and that she might even find it helpful to be free of Jamaica from time to time. An opportunity to be away from Jamaica when the inevitable blowups occurred might help to keep their relationship from deteriorating further.

Miss Pope didn't see it that way. Although she wanted Jamaica back, she was still afraid of her. She said she feared that she would not be able to get a hold on Jamaica, to make this home important and valuable to her. She wanted no outside interference. She said, "I just want Jamaica to come here and be one of us. I don't want her to have reminders of all that has happened since she was here before, and I don't want her to feel different. The other kids have no one visiting them except my family and friends, and that is what I think would be best for her too."

I pressed a bit, but it was painfully clear that Miss Pope wanted me out of the picture, that she was pushing me out: I was no longer welcome. In the back of my mind, I began to have a nagging fear. I wondered if there was anything Miss Pope was hiding, anything she was not being straight with me about. If so, it was probably best that I didn't know. My belief that her home was the only possible situation for Jamaica was strong. I didn't want to interfere in any way with that. I also was sure that Miss Pope was going to have a hard road with Jamaica and that how she wanted to travel it had to be up to her. But after all that had happened, I would miss Jamaica. I was troubled not only because I believed in the value of her having a constant friend—I had grown to like her. I had made many plans in my life around her. I would miss her a lot.

Miss Pope and I also held completely opposing views on the importance of Jamaica remembering or forgetting her past. I told Miss Pope that I felt Jamaica and I had been on a journey together. This journey had started when I met Jamaica at Mercy and had ended now that Jamaica was returning to her home. I told her that we had many memories of the things that had happened to Jamaica along the way. Some of these memories were good, some bad, but I thought it was important for Jamaica to have someone in her life who knew what had happened to her, who could share with her the memories of what her life had been. I had taken pictures of Jamaica in all the places she had lived so that she would be able to remember where she had been and the people she had met there. I told Miss Pope I would give her these pictures.

Miss Pope remained firm in her belief that the sooner Jamaica's past was forgotten and buried, the better. Though I pushed, I was not willing to challenge or antagonize her, for fear of creating strife in an already fragile situation. The last thing I wanted was an argument ending in "If you think all this is so important, and you want to keep on seeing her, then you take her—she's yours."

I suggested I call Jamaica on Saturday and talk to her on the phone to say good-bye. Miss Pope readily agreed.

I REACHED JAMAICA at the copy store. We had a brief and to the point conversation.

"Guess what, Auntie—I be comin to live wit Grandma at Christmastime. I be comin every weekend till then, when I move here. Grandma say you can't be visitin me because I be livin here now and you not my really aunt anyway. You gonna get another kid like me?"

"Slippery Shoes," I said, "there is no other kid like you. I'll miss you."

I could hear Jamaica talking to Julio. Before I could say anything else she said, "Bye, Auntie—wait for me, Julio," and ran away from the phone. I could hear the sounds of the copy shop on the other end of the line as I stood holding the phone, hoping that Jamaica would come back.

I hung up and dialed Miss Pope to tell her I hoped things would go well for her and Jamaica. I added that I thought Jamaica had grown up a bit and might behave herself at least a little. We laughed. Miss Pope said that even a little might be too much to hope for. I told her that I would be around and glad to talk if things became difficult or if she ever changed her mind and wanted a day or weekend away from Jamaica. I also told her I would send all Jamaica's photos so that she could have them for her family album. I packed them up and sent them off.

SEVERAL MONTHS PASSED. I heard nothing. Then, in April, I picked up my phone to find a furious Miss Pope on the other end. "You come get her right now or I don't know what I will do. I want her out of here now. I don't want to see that vicious little gutter rat again. Everyone was right. All she will do is bring me harm—I don't want her here anymore. Come get her and take her back to Hilltop." Miss Pope started to cry.

In a voice fueled by her rage and sense of betrayal, Miss Pope told me she had just been visited by child welfare workers to investigate charges of child abuse. The evening before, she had sent Jamaica to her room after she had drawn with a Magic Marker on the wooden living room floor, denied she had done it, and covered it up. One of the other children told Miss Pope of the misdeed. She picked up the rug and found many sexual pictures; "cunt" and "ho" were written beside women sucking breasts and penises. Stick-figure women kissed and fondled breasts. The extent of the drawing on the floor indicated it had been going on for quite a while. Miss Pope took up the rug and made Jamaica wash off all the writing, then sent her to her room. Jamaica did not cry. With one hand on her hip, she glared, then went to school the next day and rushed in to her teacher to "rat me out," as Miss Pope put it. She had told the teacher that Miss Pope hit her, made her wash floors on her hands and knees, and sometimes locked her in her room and did not give her food. Jamaica was going to be held at her school pending the result of the investigation. Miss Pope was beside herself. She had felt everything was going along well. Jamaica was in a learning-disabled class, where she seemed to be making good progress. At home she did not seem to be a discipline problem, and the fights she had in school seemed to be lessening.

"Now this bomb. Those pictures were disgusting—nothing like a young girl would even think about. Now, I don't think I can have that filthy mind working around Julio and Darius. They wouldn't even know what any of that meant. She has to get out of here before something really bad happens. Her actions not only threaten me, but Julio and Darius could be taken away, too." Miss Pope described an ominous feeling that Jamaica would do her harm. I recalled to myself what my friends had said: "She will hurt you more than you could ever hurt her."

"You can always get rid of her," I told Miss Pope. "You probably would like to kill her, but remember about her, it is not always what you do but what you have to undo that is so hard." I suggested she deal with this quickly and directly. "Go to the school and with Jamaica there talk about what happened and why you were so angry. Try to get the teacher to help you prevent Jamaica from making these accusations when she gets mad and tries to play the system off against you. I understand if you want to send her away," I said, "but if you do, she is only going to get worse, not better. We both know this is her only chance—don't give up on her yet. How about if I come over and take her for a few days? I'll be glad to. If Jamaica goes back to Hilltop, there will be no hope left for her at all."

We talked for nearly two hours. The storm passed. Miss Pope was going to go to the school after we hung up, and she was going to follow my suggestion and take Jamaica to a psychiatric clinic I knew where specialized treatment was offered to sexually abused children.

Late that evening Miss Pope called me. She had talked to the teacher in front of Jamaica, who told the teacher exactly what had happened. The teacher became Miss Pope's ally, telling Jamaica how wrong it is to falsely accuse people. If Jamaica did it again, the teacher said, she would call Miss Pope in directly. Miss Pope said she was too embarrassed to discuss the nature of the drawings. Wisely, she thought it just as well not to: she did not want to stigmatize Jamaica further.

As we were about to hang up, I asked what I had wanted to know since I last saw Jamaica. "Does she ever mention me?"

"Never has," Miss Pope replied.

"Does she still talk about her mother?"

"All the time."

Chapter 27

I thought about Jamaica less and less, but occasionally something would remind me of her—her jewelry in the piano bench, a Kentucky Fried Chicken restaurant, the book *Goodnight Moon*, the pink mug with "Jamaica" on it that sat in the back of my dish closet. Each time I saw it I wondered if one day she would reappear and want coffee with a little milk and lots of sugar. Months passed. I assumed that any news I heard would be bad, so I settled in to not wanting to hear any news at all.

Shortly before Thanksgiving of the following year, Miss Pope called again. I recognized her voice immediately and held my breath.

"Nothing bad," she said with a hearty laugh. "At least not too bad. You can relax. I'm more or less calling you for a tune-up. You said something to me once that helps when things go bad. It was that time you said, 'With Jamaica it's not what you do, but what you have to undo that makes it so hard.' Those words stuck to me. They have helped me when I've been at my wits' end. I've been doing a lot more undoing than I bargained for, but we are getting somewhere. Jamaica doesn't lie like she used to."

Miss Pope went on, "When school started this year, I went to the teacher and told her that in the past, Jamaica had told lies to get attention or to express anger with me and that if she kept on doing this she was going to lie herself right out of a good foster home. I asked the teacher to work with me, to call me in if something looked wrong, if Jamaica said anything or acted up in ways to cause her alarm.

"No sooner had I said this than the teacher called to ask if Jamaica was pregnant. I nearly fell out. All I could think was, 'Dear God, not this—who could it be?' I couldn't imagine Jamaica having been with any man, but knowing Jamaica I did wonder if she picked up someone, if there was someone in the neighborhood, if she had snuck out like she does. But I could not imagine how or when. Then I realized that this skinny little girl has not even had her period. I didn't think it physically possible. Still I fretted and worried myself all the way to the school. Jamaica was waiting with the teacher in the nurse's office. I went on in there, saw that child sitting calmly eating a bag of chips and I blew.

" 'Jamaica, just what are you telling your teacher?'

" 'I jus be playin, Grandma.'

" 'Playin what?'

"Jamaica looked down at the floor. She did not want to answer me, so I went right up to her, took her chin in my hand, and said, 'Now, you look right at me, child, and you tell me exactly what you told your teacher, because I am not playing with you. I am serious and I am upset, so you better stop your playing and tell all of us here what is going on.'

" 'I wuz jus playin wit my teacher, Grandma, so I toll her I wuz gonna have a baby. I wanna see how she react. She say, "What?" She look surprise an so I say, "Yep, I be gonna have a baby an me an my baby gonna live wit Grandma, so I kin still come to school an be in your class and all." Then the teacher look upset an send me here. The nurse ax is it true that I'm gonna have a baby. I say it is true an that you like babies so we gonna live wit you. Then the nurse say stay in this room an she gonna call you to come get me. Then some mans come to ask me if I'm gonna have a baby.

I tell him yes, too. He say am I sure and I say, "Yep, I know I'm gonna have a baby." '

" 'What made you think of having a baby?' I asked.

" 'Jus playin—I jus thought it.'

" 'Jamaica,' the nurse asked, 'are you having a baby?'

"Jamaica frowned and shook her head from side to side. She would not look me in my eye.

"Then the nurse asked if Jamaica knew how girls got pregnant.

"Jamaica replied, 'I be knowin that my whole life.'

"I stood Jamaica up, told her I wanted her to apologize to these people for lying to them and playing with them in a way to cause trouble. I wanted her to know in front of the teacher, nurse, and principal that we all took this very seriously. I told them if Jamaica came in to tell tales, I wanted to be called immediately. I said that Jamaica has done this before and that if she wants to continue to live with me, she has to stop doing it. This is going to be the last time. I was glad to have all those witnesses to the way she can make up a story just like that.

"I also said that I wanted to tell Jamaica right in front of everyone so that Jamaica will always remember that I said it: if Jamaica ever gets pregnant when she is living in my house, out she goes. I will not keep her and I will not keep any baby. If Jamaica wants to stay with me she goes to school and learns something. If she fools around and gets herself pregnant, she will be leaving my house forever. I will never take her back.

"Right then I wished I knew somebody with a baby I could borrow to make Jamaica change dirty diapers for a week or two. That would be good punishment. Maybe that would cure her of her lying about babies.

"After all that, the school made me get her a pregnancy test. It came back negative. Jamaica told me that she had not had sex with anyone since she lived with her mother. I believe that is true, but I also see how much she is thinking about sex. She will be lucky to make fifteen without being pregnant. This made me really stop and think about what will happen in the future when she does get her period and can get pregnant.

"I have been thinking that the best thing for me to do is to take these children and move back down south to Georgia where my brother lives. Everything is easier there. The schools don't have shootings and drugs, and the children are not so wild and crazy. People have families. My brother owns a small restaurant where I could work and get on my feet. He wants me to come, and I think it would be good for all the kids to have a man around, certainly for Darius and Julio, but mostly for Jamaica. He has met the kids. He likes Jamaica, thinks she has a lot of spirit. He can be tough—he was with his own kids. Jamaica needs that, someone who will take none of her nonsense.

"I can't just up and go yet because of foster care. My caseworker told me there is a provision where you can adopt and receive benefits for caring for the child just like in foster care. But because they are your kids, you can move wherever you have to go. I had started looking into that for all three kids when another crisis occurred. This time Jamaica had nothing to do with making the problem.

"Part of the plan for my leaving was that my son would take over the house, pay the mortgage, and eventually pay me back. He and his wife moved in with their children so that I could go to Georgia for three weeks to look around for a place for us to live. While I was away, a welfare worker representing Julio and Darius's mother, who is in the process of giving up her parental rights, came to make a visit. When she found that I was gone without permission and that my son, who has no license for foster care, was taking care of the kids she hit the roof and called her supervisor, who called the Bureau of Child Welfare. Before my son and daughter-in-law could even contact me, the children were moved to temporary foster homes way up in the Bronx. Jamaica went to one, Julio and Darius to another.

"The children were frantic, I was frantic, my son was so furious he even tried to call the police to prevent them from taking the children until I could fly back to straighten things out. He was beside himself that they did not look at the fact that he is a college graduate who holds a decent job and has never been in one bit of trouble. Truth is, I never thought such a thing could happen. I feel so much that these kids are part of the family, I just went on vacation like anyone would do and planned with my son and his wife to care for the kids. She loves the kids. She tried to get an emergency license to hold our family together, but they wouldn't give it to her.

"All three of the kids were a mess, but, as you can imagine, Jamaica caused the most trouble. She is tough and was so determined to come back that she kept running away. The first time she was picked up by the police in the Bronx and sent to Mercy. She ran away from there—stole the wallet of an aide to get subway money. She got hopelessly lost in the subway and was picked up by the transit police. By then I was back, trying to find the kids. Darius was really hurt—he is a fragile child anyway. With strangers in a new home, he would not talk at all. They told me he became catatonic and was on his way to the child ward at Montefiore Hospital when I went to visit him. He clung to my leg for all he was worth. I told him I was trying to get him back, but he was inconsolable.

"Finally, a hearing was held. I was given a warning not to leave without permission again, and all the children were returned to me. All that could have been avoided with just a few phone calls. But, as you well know, that's not the way things work. It seems the sensible never happens. Jamaica nearly got herself into juvenile detention, she was so wild and uncontrollable. This time I can't blame her. Maybe, if I was as tough as her, I might have done the same.

"What happened just put another scar on them. I was trying to give them security that nothing would happen while I was in charge, but I missed one move and it all came falling down. I'll keep trying to adopt them if I can get the subsidy—that way they'll be mine and I can guarantee them something."

As Miss Pope talked, I wondered once again whether there was some mystery in her life, whether there was something hidden going on that I sensed sometimes but could not put my finger on. My own experience with Jamaica had taught me that the child welfare system was callous and that defeat was possible at every step of the way despite effort and the best intentions. I also knew that it was hard to impart a sense of security when you did not have control over what plans you could make for a child. What had happened to Miss Pope had happened to me. Someone with power could countermand your plans, and you were helpless.

But something still nagged at me about Miss Pope. There was a lot I didn't know about her. I never stopped wondering if she had had a hidden reason for not wanting me around. Clearly, she liked to talk to me on the phone. She called for help when things got rough. I thought probably she did know she wasn't allowed to leave the children with someone who wasn't certified—likely she took a chance and got caught. I recalled that when I'd first gotten in touch with her, she hadn't wanted Jamaica to come visit without being properly signed out, lest that jeopardize her foster care of Darius and Julio. She was aware of those rules.

I was troubled by what had just happened and hoped I had done the right thing for Jamaica. Throughout my relationship with Jamaica, her precarious status had led me to back away from many disputes or problems when I felt confronting them might result in more loss for her. Once, Miss Pope had called to ask me to pick up two tickets to *Cats* for her daughter's birthday. Since I was in the city, I could buy them on the way to get Jamaica and bring her back to Hilltop. The two tickets cost $100. Miss Pope knew this, because she had told me the location of the seats she wanted and how much she wanted to pay. She said clearly that she would give me $100 when I came to her house.

I picked Jamaica up, gave Miss Pope the tickets, and put the folded bills into my pocket. When I got home, there were three twenties. I fished in my pocket, counted the money over and over, wrapped and unwrapped it. Had I dropped the money, was this an oversight, had one of the children taken the money, should I call her? If I did, would she be insulted? Did this mean anything at all? I left it alone, as one of the things I would never know. Whatever irregularities there might be in Miss Pope's life, I knew I wanted to leave them be. The stakes were enormous, the facts undeniable: Miss Pope's home offered more to Jamaica than anything else in sight.

"I knew you'd be interested to know that things are never calm around here. But they are not as bad as they could be. Jamaica missed getting into worse trouble by a hair. What is it they say about a miss being like a mile? She is still with me, not back in some institution or kids' jail. That child seems to have those nine cat lives—I hope they are not tested again."

Miss Pope did plan to move to Georgia, her brother had a job waiting for her, and she could live with him until she found a place for herself and the three children. She had moved to adopt all three. Whatever problems there might be in this home, these good things applied.

I missed Jamaica and felt a longing to protect her. I could only imagine her fear when she ran away and raced down unfamiliar streets, searching wildly and without direction for the way back to Miss Pope and the home that, despite this latest setback, was beginning to seem as if it really would be hers.

"Is Jamaica home now?" I asked. "I'd love to speak to her."

"Jamaica!" Miss Pope yelled. "Come here, child—someone wants to speak to you."

I heard the familiar deep, throaty hello.

"Jamaica," I said, "do you know who this is?"

Without missing a beat, Jamaica replied, "And you be sayin it was jus heat lightnin—thas what you be sayin."

"We didn't melt or wash away."

"No, but I be freezin my butt until you put me in that hot shower an all. Remember how you had to put all those towels aroun me an even had to make me a hood an put my butt in front of the fire?"

I could imagine Jamaica on the other end of the phone looking very serious as she shook her head in disdain at my stupidity. I was pleased at her recognition of that shared intimacy and was glad Jamaica had the memory of it. I hoped she had some other memories that brought her the pleasure they brought me when I recalled them.

"I hear you may be moving down South, where Grandma's brother lives."

"His name be Robbie—he like me a lot an he be really fine. Grandma say we be gettin our own house down there, but first we be livin with Robbie. Thas okay wit me, cause I love Robbie an I hope we can stay wit him for a long time."

"I hope you all will like it there," I told Jamaica, knowing that she had likely reached the end of her endurance for phone conversations.

"Okay, Auntie, bye," she said before I could finish my sentence.

Miss Pope took back the phone. "I don't expect we'll be able to leave for a few months, but I'll let you know before we go what has happened with the adoption and where we'll be living in Georgia. I know you would like to see Jamaica again—and now," she said, in what seemed to be a change of mind, "I think that would be a good thing too."

"I'd love to see her again," I replied. "Before I forget how to deal with all her maneuvers and get myself into trouble."

"Don't worry, I have lots of practice, and I'll be right here to remind you," Miss Pope said. She hung up the phone.

That night I had a dream:

My doorbell rang. I looked out the window and saw a man standing at the bottom of the steps. A fat young woman was coming up the steps, lugging two huge green garbage bags. I went to the door and saw Jamaica. She was older now and had dyed her hair platinum blond. I knew it was Jamaica, but she said her name was Lanie. She had all her belongings in these two huge garbage bags. She had come to live with me. No one had called me—why was she here? I looked at the bottom of the steps; the man had left without a word. I told her to come in. I knew she couldn't stay with us. What was I going to do? Lanie told me she was bleeding, that she had her period. I saw the blood and wondered if she had napkins in the garbage bags. I did not want her to get blood all over the sheets. I knew it was Jamaica, but her face was so bloated it was hard to find her features. Where could I bring her back to? They had just dumped her here. I stared. I saw something move in the garbage bag.

I woke up, frightened that Jamaica would have a baby soon. If she got pregnant, I wondered, would she stay with Grandma or be kicked out? Could she find me if she wanted to? If she did, what would I do? She might not know or remember my last name. I had taught her my address when she was at Mercy, but did she still remember? I thought of possible landmarks and wondered if she had a map in her head from Mercy or the Bagel Shop.

What would happen to the baby?

Chapter 28

Over five years have passed. I've heard nothing. I've sent Christmas cards each year to both Miss Pope and Jamaica. My return address, printed boldly on the left-hand corner of the envelope, has not returned the cards to me.

One day last fall, I picked up phone messages in my office and heard, "Please call Miss Higby at Hilltop School."

I was late for my next appointment, but I dialed the number anxiously, expecting that surely this would be news of Jamaica. Partly I felt raw white fear that something terrible had happened to her.

"Miss Atkins, do you know who this is?" Miss Higby inquired.

"How could I forget? What is the news of Jamaica?"

"That's what we would like to know. Neither we nor any of the agencies that have been involved with her know anything about where she is or what has happened to her. We were going through old records up here, trying to update and document what has happened to some of the children who passed through the school. We remember Jamaica vividly. She was so wild and plain bad. We came to her name and everyone wanted to know about her, yet we had no knowledge, not a trace of information, and no leads. I said to the director that there was one person who always kept track of her, one person who really liked her, who fought for her and always showed up. I remember our conniving together to get her into foster care, so I figured you would know how she is doing."

"I wish I did," I replied. "The last I knew, she was going to be adopted by Miss Pope and move to Georgia. As far as I know this is what happened, but I can't be sure because I haven't heard a word from Miss Pope for over five years. I know the plan was for Miss Pope to move to Georgia and for her son and grandchildren to remain in her house. I'm sure her son could tell us Miss Pope's whereabouts. I'd love an excuse to call. I'll be glad to do it."

I told Miss Higby I would call back with whatever information I was able to find.

As I looked through my old address book for Miss Pope's phone number, I was aware of the long estrangement. The phone number was familiar. I dialed it, tense with anticipation of who might answer.

"This is the Center for Asian Technology," an accented voice announced.

"I must have the wrong number," I replied.

I checked the number in my book and tried it again. Again the same response.

I checked Information. No number, listed or unlisted, for either Miss Pope or her son. No listing in any of the boroughs, or in the town in Georgia where Miss Pope had planned to move. I did not know her brother's last name.

"Can't you have the computer look up adoption records or call the child protective services you turned her case over to?" I asked Miss Higby. "Perhaps they will know whether Jamaica was adopted and where she has gone."

"We don't want to know *that* bad," Miss Higby replied. "We were sitting around in the office talking about different kids we had known here. Jamaica came up. We recalled that she had no relatives or anyone but you who had any connection to her. We became curious about how things had gone for her. It was more curiosity than actual information we need to have. Sometimes no news is good news. If something terrible happened to her, we'd probably find out when someone investigated her past. This may be the best thing."

"You mean I'll know what happened to her if she gets dumped in a river, but not if she finishes high school? If you'll look up the foster care agency that took charge of her placement, I'll call them and see if they can tell me what has happened. If she was adopted and the agency is still paying for her care in Georgia, they should have the address."

"I'm sorry I got you on the track of wanting to know," Miss Higby said.

"I've never stopped wanting to know," I replied.

"We can't be of any help. We're really short-staffed now, and by law I can't give you that kind of information anyway, even if I could find it. If I hear anything I'll call you."

I hung up. Once again I felt the helplessness I had so often felt in my experiences with Jamaica. I was in the same position I had always been in with her. I have no right to know anything. In the absence of knowing, I can only imagine.

I can imagine Jamaica now. If her life is going well, perhaps that husky voice belts out from the choir loft of the church that she and Miss Pope attend together in her small southern town. Perhaps by now she has her own dog to walk or cat to pet. Maybe she rollerblades around the sidewalks and runs home from school to a house and room she loves and can stay in day after day, month after month, year after year. Perhaps her name is Pope now and Grandma is a "really" relative. Together they drink coffee with a little milk and lots of sugar, and nobody can tell them not to. Maybe she has learned to read a bit better; maybe she will finish high school and have her own junior prom, where she will wear a fancy dress that Grandma has made for her. A boy will put a flower on her wrist, and she and the friends she now has will dance nonstop all night long. I wonder if her school has a track team. I know she will win sometimes if she is on it. I imagine she watches a lot of television and rents horror movies whenever she can. She probably still glares defiantly and shakes her head in disgust at other people's stupidity and at things that rub her the wrong way.

Perhaps the ordinary has become her pleasure to enjoy each day, without insult to her or the threat of loss through no fault of her own. Perhaps she can now hold on to, keep, take for granted, even cherish and feel part of a family who will laugh at her jokes and be happy when she walks through the door.

I hope for her. But at unguarded and unanticipated moments I know that it is a hope without strong conviction. A short time ago, when I was headed uptown on the subway, something across the tracks caught my eye. I glanced over. There, sitting on the dank concrete platform, her back nestled into the hollow of a steel beam, a small, thin, dirty form in a blue sweatshirt held out a cupped hand to the passersby. I saw Jamaica's hand—shiny, light brown, thin, bony little fingers. The head was small, the hair short and matted. The face was visible for just a second, until a train whizzed by to block my view. But I thought I saw Jamaica's face, the eyes narrowed, the defiance glowering. I raced up the stairs and down the other side. There, sitting in dirty, crusted black jeans, her head nodding, her baby tucked under her knees, a young woman begged. Her face turned real to me. The face was not Jamaica's, but it seemed to embody Jamaica's history. The words she spoke, which stayed with me as I walked away from the outstretched begging hand, could have been Jamaica's words—her inimitable turn of phrase.

"A penny for my thoughts?"

In the years I knew Jamaica, we had a moment together. What happened in that moment gave Jamaica her only shot. She knew it, I knew it, Miss Pope knew it. And although the alignment was never perfect, and it was not, in the end, the way I would have had us go, a strange alchemy brought all of us to line up together toward an imperfect and shaky target. I only hope that Jamaica has been able to stand upright through the buffeting of her own chaos, and that the prevailing winds of her misfortunes have not been powerful enough to once again blow blinding sand back in her face.

And I hope that one day I will see her again.

Acknowledgments

A book—like a child—needs a nurturing, faithful family in order to thrive, to grow. *Jamaica and Me* has been lucky—it has had two such families. To the godparents, Linda Wells and Jerome Charyn, who shepherded the book through its early life, I am deeply grateful. To Daniel Menaker and Gail Hochman, the foster parents, who continued to look after the book as it grew, my gratitude is enormous.

To Linda Wells, thank you for your instant response and unbridled enthusiasm.

To Daniel Menaker, I could neither have dreamed of nor have wished for a wiser, more psychologically astute, or more compassionate editor.

To Gail Hochman, my literary agent—from the beginning you have given me and the book a safe and loving literary home at Brandt & Brandt.

To Jerome Charyn, there will never be enough gratitude for your friendship, support, and protection. Your keen eye and well-tuned ear helped me to open pathways into my own heart.

To all the members of the Island Writers' Workshop, my gratitude for the gifts of your writing and your dreams.

About the Author

LINDA ATKINS is a practicing psychoanalyst
with a master's degree in clinical social work
from Columbia University and a degree in the
psychoanalytical treatment of children from the
Jewish Board of Family Services. She
completed psychoanalytic training for work
with adults at the Postgraduate Center for
Mental Health, where she now teaches,
supervises, and holds the position of training
analyst. She has won several awards for her
professional publications.

Born in Boston, Linda Atkins has been a
New Yorker for over thirty years. She has
worked as a volunteer with several children in
institutions and in agencies concerned with
children's lives. She has two children and
currently lives in Greenwich Village with her
husband.

About the Type

The text of this book was set in Janson, a
misnamed typeface designed in about 1690 by
Nicholas Kis, a Hungarian in Amsterdam. In
1919 the matrices became the property of the
Stempel Foundry in Frankfurt. It is an old-style
book face of excellent clarity and sharpness.
Janson serifs are concave and splayed; the
contrast between thick and thin strokes is
marked.